BHS TREC

BHS TREC

British Horse Society
Reg. Charity No. 210504

Robert Jones

KENILWORTH PRESS

First published in 2005 by
Kenilworth Press Ltd
Addington
Buckingham MK18 2JR

British Library Cataloguing in Publication Data
A catalogue record for this book is available from the British Library

ISBN 1-872119-91-3

Layout by Kenilworth Press
Printed in Malta on behalf of Compass Press

AUTHOR'S NOTE

In all instances the use of the word 'horse' equally denotes pony.

Contents

ILLUSTRATION CREDITS

Diagrams
Map illustrations: **Dianne Breeze**
S-bend layout: **Michael J. Stevens**

Photographs
Patrick Stubbs (Natural Expressions Photography): pages 2, 18, 20, 23, 29, 35, 36, 37, 69, 71, 74, 76
Other photos supplied by Robert Jones, Robert Weatherly, Denos Constantine, Robert Billson, Heather Lucas, and Chris Smalley

Introduction

THE PRIME AIM OF THIS BOOK is to explain clearly and simply how to take part in TREC competitions. It covers the basic skills you will need to have, or to develop, to enable you to enjoy the event and be effective. It includes some tips to help you prepare for your first event, covers the equipment that you will require, describes each of the three phases in detail, and has some specific advice about training for the PTV obstacles.

You will get the maximum benefit from the book if you use it in conjunction with the official *BHS TREC Rulebook*, as this text does not aim to interpret every nuance of every rule.

This book also gives you a brief insight into the history and development of TREC, and its introduction into Great Britain by The British Horse Society (BHS). It also discusses the philosophy behind the sport and its link to the whole area of equestrian tourism.

There were a number of reasons why the BHS decided to introduce TREC into Great Britain. Within the Society there had long been a belief that there was a demand for a general organised riding activity, not necessarily of a competitive nature, aimed at the group of riders broadly described as recreational riders. As far as it is possible to identify this group, they are riders across the complete range of abilities for whom riding is principally a pastime, rather than a profession. Their chief motivation for riding has far more to do with personal achievement and the satisfaction of developing a closer relationship with their horse than with winning, although this is not meant to suggest that they cannot be fiercely competitive. Nor is it meant to suggest that any of the other disciplines of riding and driving do not allow individuals to develop unique relationships with their horses, or that they are in any way less sympathetic to the horse. However, it is clear that a very significant number of riders are not motivated to take part in what could best be described as our traditional and established sporting disciplines. The reasons range from lack of time for training, insufficient funds, unsuitable horses, demanding and stressful jobs, and, in some instances, ability, as these sports become more and more demanding.

TREC was also seen as satisfying the Society's underlying objectives. It was aimed at, and was accessible to, the majority of people who ride in Great Britain, including non horse owners. It was as inexpensive as any horse sport could reasonably expect to be. It had implications with regard to developing basic skills within the riding community across a very broad range, with similar implications for the training of horses, without the emphasis being solely on a sporting outcome.

TREC required many more riders to become aware of the problems and political issues surrounding the question of access to the countryside for riders and carriage drivers and helped to develop an understanding of the economic importance of access for tourism. The underlying principles behind the preparation of horses and riders for competition puts great emphasis on the safety and welfare of both while they enjoy 'outdoor riding', and it put an additional marketing tool into the hands of riding schools, especially the smaller, more generalist, rurally based ones.

The Society continues to back the development of TREC for these reasons, and to motivate many more people to work with, and join, the BHS.

A Brief History

Although TREC is not an old sport in comparison with many equestrian disciplines, its precise origins are still not easy to pinpoint. The sport began in France; of that there appears to be no doubt, but the sport did not spring into being from a single idea. It developed gradually from a number of separate activities, and with a particular philosophy about the sympathetic use of the horse in 'nature', fitting into the natural environment as unobtrusively as possible.

In France, the growth of the equestrian tourism industry was encouraged by the government as one of the ways in which it hoped to regenerate its rural economy, which had been shattered by the Second World War. Government support was given to tourism of any description (whether on foot, bicycle or on horse-back), and the development of a professional workforce for this sector of the industry was encouraged. Vocational qualifications for the equestrian tourism industry were established and professionals began to develop tourism with horses and associated activities.

It is unlikely that TREC was introduced formally as a means of testing the skills of professional trail guides (known as *accompagnateurs*) in France. A much more likely origin links TREC to the development of the Equirando, which began life as a *rallye nationale* in 1961. The Equirando has now evolved into a festival for equestrian tourists who gather in a different town in France each year, for three days of what can be best described as partying with their horses and ponies. Today, this event requires all the participants to ride to the venue from their respective homes, and each year there is a prize for the person who travels the furthest. Often the winner of this award will have travelled six or seven hundred kilometres to reach the Equirando, but it will probably be a long time before anyone matches the feat of a rider from Kiev who covered over 3,200 km to get there!

During the Equirando, any number of events and displays might take place including a TREC competition and guided pleasure rides. In fact, just about any activity that it is reasonable to imagine doing with horses and ponies, whether ridden or driven. In the recent past, even riders from Britain have crossed the Channel to join in, and similar events have sprung up in other countries on the Continent, most notably in Italy, but we have yet to reproduce our own version of the Equirando in Great Britain. In its most popular years, the Equirando can attract upwards of 1,200 horses.

However, its origins were a far cry from the large event that the Equirando has now become. Beginning as an annual gathering for equestrian tourists, professional trail guides were included, keen no doubt to share ideas and experiences and to contemplate future developments soberly over a glass or two of wine! It became one of the features of these gatherings that the guides demonstrated the particular strengths and abilities of their own horses, whether it be in dealing with problems encountered on the trail, reaching a destination at the expected time or even such a simple thing as showing which horse could canter slower than all the others or walk more quickly. Indeed, the times achieved during these particular gatherings were subsequently to set the standards for the Control of Paces (*Maîtrise des Allures*) in TREC competitions.

As these 'demonstrations' took on a more formal structure, the concept of a number of different competitions based around all these skills took shape, in which the idea of TREC was born. Initially, separate events developed. Long orienteering events, of which the Centaure Bourgogne (an annual event in Burgundy, run over two nights and covering 100 km) is a current example, took place, normally over two days, with competitors expected to cover 150 km. A separate Parcours du Cavalier et du Cheval de Randonnée (competition for rider and horse used for tourism) developed and this in due course would become the PTV phase in TREC; but it wasn't until 1980 that a national event involving the three phases of today's TREC competitions took place at Fontainebleau. In 1987 the sport took on the title of T.R.E.C. – Techniques de Randonnée Equestre de Compétition.

By the time the first World Championships took place, TREC was firmly established as a competitive discipline in many countries on the Continent. France, Italy, Spain, Germany, Switzerland, Austria and Belgium began regularly contesting European Championships run under the rules of the Fédération Internationale de Tourisme Equestre (FITE), established in 1975. In 1996, during the 12th European Championships, the General Assembly of FITE took the decision to hold a World Championships the following year in France, hoping to attract riders from three continents, as TREC had begun to take place in the old French colonies in North Africa and in Quebec.

The General Assembly also expressed the hope that Great Britain would join the Championships. This was by no means the first time that Great Britain had been invited to join in competition. In 1988, an invitation had been extended to attend the European Championships taking place that year in Fontainebleu. No team went, but Janet Miller from Surrey borrowed her daughter's event horse and set off across the Channel. Janet had a thoroughly enjoyable time and was made royally welcome (as is usually the case with any British competitor who ventures abroad), and on her return made a sterling effort to set TREC up in this country.

For a year or two, Janet ran a version of TREC, which she called Equi-cross, in the South East. The competitions were well supported but, with only one person promoting the concept, regardless of how hard they worked, it stood little chance of expanding beyond the confines of Surrey. It was not until 1998 that a concerted effort was made by a national organisation to introduce TREC formally to this country, and even then it took two years from considering the idea to actually mounting an event.

Prior to this, in 1995 the BHS had become a full member of FITE, principally to develop qualifications appropriate for the equestrian tourism industry in Britain and to gain international recognition for those qualifications. A number of organisations had been working together to develop qualifications for this sector of the industry and in 1995 the first British Equestrian Tourism (BET) certificates (see Appendix 4) were awarded by the President of FITE at a ceremony in London. The potential of TREC had still not really intruded into the development plans of the Society.

However, in the autumn of that year, a representative of the BHS attended the annual General Assembly of FITE, which coincided with the 12th European Championships being held at El Montanya, the site of the 1992 Olympic Three-Day Event. Invited to remain as an observer for the competition, and receiving every offer of help to encourage the sport in Britain, he subsequently presented a positive report of TREC to the BHS initially to the Training and Education Committee. Under the guidance of the Head of Training and Education, John Goldsmith, the go-ahead was given to research TREC and look at the possibilities and practicalities of introducing the sport to Britain. Naturally, that was easier said than done.

In order to discover more about TREC, it was necessary for British riders to take part in a competition abroad. This seemed the best way to obtain an insider's view of the competition and to discover if these riders thought the competition would be transferable to this country. It was

Saint Pierre d'Albigny, venue for the first World Championships.

decided that it would be worthwhile sending a team to represent Great Britain in what was to be the first TREC World Championships in September 1997, taking place at Saint Pierre d'Albigny in the French Alps. To have attempted to do this in any of the other equestrian disciplines would have been considered perfectly insane, but the BHS was confident that the team could deal with the riding demands of the competition, even on borrowed horses, and the worst that could go wrong was they would get a bit lost in France!

The Society sought suitable riders from within the equestrian tourism industry as being the people most likely to be in touch with the likes and dislikes of the rider market that TREC would appeal to. It was also felt that the holiday riding centres would be the driving force behind any attempt to introduce TREC into Britain, and that those already working in this sector of the industry were most likely to have the skills to cope with the demands of such a Championships. It was also agreed to try to recruit the team from across England, Scotland and Wales to make the dissemination of news about TREC easier.

In the end, the team consisted of a rider from Wales (Paul Turner), one from Scotland (Kevin Galbraith), an Englishman living in France (Simon Zapata), who was the only experienced TREC competitor, and three riders from England (Fiona Lockhart, Nicky Hewer and team captain Bob Weatherley). Their views would determine whether any attempt would be made to promote TREC in Britain.

The competition, for which they had just four days to prepare, was far more challenging than anyone had anticipated. The first day (the map-reading phase known as the POR) was long, technically difficult and arduous. The first rider set off in the dark, with the added bonus of a thick mist to help matters along, and the last two of our riders finished in the dark. All had found the going tough, but the majority view was that it was mentally exhausting and great fun!

The riders all coped with the second day, which placed the emphasis on riding skills, without too many problems, although they had not had the opportunity to gain an intimate knowledge of the basis for the judging (rather crucial in a competition at this level). However, the really important result was that they had all enjoyed the experience and thought that it was a sport that British riders would take to.

From the team point of view the competition result was an irrelevance, but suffice it to say the French were convincing winners. Great Britain was not disgraced, managing to beat some of the established teams who were riding their own horses. The USA, who were going through the same exercise with a team of students from Averett College in North Carolina, also came out of the Championships with honour intact.

The feedback from this fact-finding mission was crucially important and confirmed that this was a sport that could be transplanted to Britain. The BHS now had the tools with which to publicise TREC. The Society then embarked on a campaign to introduce the idea of TREC into this country, initially through its series of regional conferences for proprietors of riding schools. The reaction was lukewarm to start with, and it was not until the conference for Scotland at Oatridge College in the spring of 1998 that the idea took hold.

There can be little doubt that the potential of TREC in terms of business promotion lay behind the interest, coupled with an immediate identification of the skills necessary to take part in the sport, and within days of the conference at Oatridge College in 1998, Jacqueline Rider from Glen Tanar Equestrian Centre near Aberdeen was in touch with the BHS, proposing a date for the first ever TREC competition in Britain run under FITE rules. The event was to be supported by the local authority, the local tourist board and, crucially, supported financially by Sport Scotland. The event went ahead in May of that year in the beautiful wooded hills of the Glen Tanar Estate, with riders from all over Scotland taking part, and even a few travelling up from England and Wales to participate. The hard work of all those involved with the organisation of the event paid off, and BHS TREC, as a sporting discipline, was given the very best of starts.

Two more highly successful events took place in that year, one at Glen Tanar and one at Kelburn Park on the other side of Scotland. Both events attracted riders from France, who were full of praise for the running of the

competition and offered invaluable advice to help the BHS and organisers of individual competitions plan for the future. The French team was
able to warn against the mistake that had affected France, where too much
emphasis had been placed on competitions at the highest level and the
bedrock of competition had been neglected. Since then the BHS has
always tried to maintain a balance of difficulty in the range of competitions taking place, giving those new to the sport plenty of opportunities
to enter at the starter level (Level 1) while looking to develop suitably
taxing events up to Level 4 to hone the skills and competitive edge of those
seeking a higher degree of challenge, and offer them the opportunity to
gain experience in preparation for international events.

The following year, the first training courses for judges were held,
drawing on expertise from abroad with FITE trainers coming from Italy
and France, giving Britain the opportunity to develop a cadre of internationally qualified judges, who were then able to pass their knowledge onto
a wider audience.

Since then, progress has been rapid, with events running throughout
Great Britain and across all the official BHS levels (see Appendix 1). With
an average of fifty competitions a year, and in the region of 2,500 starters,
BHS TREC has become firmly established in the equestrian calendar.
Four domestic Championship events (Wales, Scotland, England and
Great Britain) are now a regular feature of the TREC calendar each year
and include classes for individuals, pairs and young riders (16–21 years)
across the levels with the exception of Level 1.

In just six years Great Britain established itself as one of the strongest
competitive nations in the world, having won two team silver medals (in
2001 and 2003), and individual gold (David Hay-Thorburn in 2000) in
the Senior World Championships by 2003. A European Young Riders'
Championships was introduced in 2001 and by 2003 Great Britain had
won an individual silver (Rebecca Hine in 2001), an individual gold (Kate
Ellison in 2003) and a team bronze (2003).

In 2005, a European Cup competition was introduced by FITE,
which can briefly be described as a league event for individual riders, with
the results determined by performance in four designated international
competitions.

The sport goes from strength to strength, as each year more riders discover a sporting challenge that matches their competitive aspirations to a
desire to develop a closer understanding and working relationship with
their equine partners. The prospect for the future looks very bright.

PART ONE

TREC EXPLAINED

CHAPTER ONE

What is TREC?

T REC AS A SPORTING DISCIPLINE is about what horses are really good at
– being a versatile, multi talented, intelligent, safe, efficient means of
transport. Even this explanation ignores what for most riders is the more
important aspect of the sport, the opportunity it gives them to develop a
closer relationship with their horse. While most of the riders do enjoy the
competitive element of an event, for many the greater appeal of TREC is
the opportunity it gives them to ride in different, and often beautiful,
parts of the countryside, and to meet a number of varied challenges, both
physical and intellectual.

Put in very simple terms, TREC is a competition that examines the
horse and rider in a situation with which they should be very familiar –
hacking through the countryside without getting lost, and dealing with
the sort of problems and hazards they would be likely to come across.
However, as you might expect, there is far more to it than at first appears.

In terms of horsemanship, TREC requires the rider to develop a very
broad range of basic skills, and to focus on doing them very well. An
element of this may sound contradictory but so often in sport, not just
riding, we lose sight of doing the basic and simple things well. In a search
for sporting perfection we may be encouraged to over-complicate the
endeavour or attempt things that are beyond our abilities or the abilities
of our horses. The result can be demoralising and depressing. We lack
pride in doing the simple things well, and retreat into the ' I don't do anything with my horse, just hack' apology. Many give the impression that
they feel lesser riders as a result, and feel that they are looked down on by
the greater part of the equestrian industry.

Given the physiological make-up of equines, getting them to go out

Facing page:
PTV – An artificial
water crossing in
the 2003 Young
Riders' European
Championships in
Belgium.

POR – 'Are you sure this is the right way?'

on their own away from the comfort of the herd and, while on the road, face the most intimidating, fast, uncaring predator of all, the motor vehicle, should be seen as an outstanding personal achievement. In terms of courage, both for horse and rider, it should be remembered that statistically going out for a hack is the most dangerous thing a rider can do with a horse. But we all do it without generally giving it an apprehensive thought, and usually without any training.

How much better for us all – horse, rider and any other user of the outdoor environment if we were to train ourselves and our horses specifically to deal with this challenge. TREC sets out to motivate people to do just this. But it can be far more than a sporting discipline and the motivating force to focus on a broad range of basic skills in training the horse and rider. It can be the inspiration to open up a whole new range of activities for the 'average' rider quite outside the competitive environment. The competition is aimed at giving the rider and the horse the confidence and ability to cope with most of the surprises and challenges which riding in the outdoors can spring on them. With this confidence and ability comes greater safety for the partnership, a greater understanding of the physical and psychological demands placed on horses in this environment, coupled with an ecological, historical and social appreciation of the countryside.

TREC may even motivate some to consider undertaking much larger projects than the increasingly popular activity of taking one's horse on holiday to ride and explore unfamiliar areas of the country. Unknown to most of us, there are individuals all over the world undertaking what are generally known as 'long rides'. These intrepid individuals are making journeys on horseback covering thousands of kilometres over many months, if not years. While few of us can ever hope to emulate them, reading about their experiences is fascinating and very illuminating. There is a great deal the TREC competitor can learn from the experiences of these people and how they deal with problems, and their information about equipment can be extremely useful. It is well worth having a look at the website of the Long Riders' Guild (www.thelongridersguild.com) to find out about this world of equestrian adventure.

PHASES

The TREC competition usually runs in three phases (it is not unusual to find the order of the phases switched around particularly with a one-day competition), with the outcome determined by the accumulation of points.

The first phase, known by its French title – *Parcours d'Orientation et de Regularité* (POR) is basically described as orienteering on horseback. Competitors are required to follow precisely a route that they have marked on a map and this route can vary from 7 or 8 kilometres (km) up to 45 km depending on the level of competition. A number of checkpoints are included on the route, and these serve to check competitors' times, that they are following the route accurately, and that the horse is in good physical condition. The number and whereabouts of these checkpoints is unknown to the competitors. Between these checkpoints, set speeds are imposed by the organiser so, in addition to following the route accurately, competitors must try to complete each stage as near to the optimum time as possible.

Each competitor in an individual class begins this phase with 240 points, and penalties are deducted from this total for straying from the correct route, and for finishing the stage too quickly or too slowly. During this phase, the competitor can also lose points for not carrying the required equipment (see section on equipment), and in higher level competitions being held back at the equine fitness inspection.

The vast majority of events include classes for pairs. The rules for pairs classes are normally identical to the individual class, except that two competitors ride the POR together. They would finish this phase on the same score, and would go on to ride the other phases in the same way as an individual. Their collective score determines their placing. These classes are for those who enjoy company when out on a hack, or to enable riders under sixteen to compete with an older partner. BHS TREC rules do not allow someone under sixteen to tackle the POR alone.

The second phase is a test of the rider's ability to influence the horse's paces and is known as the Control of Gaits or Paces. The competitor is required to demonstrate the degree of control that he or she has while first cantering, and then walking along a marked course up to 150 m in length. The objective of this test is that the partnership should canter the course slowly, and walk quickly while always maintaining the required gait. Points to be added to the score from Phase 1 are calculated against a time chart (see Appendix 2).

The third and final phase is again known by its French name – the *Parcours en Terrain Varié* (PTV) and it bears a similarity to a hunter trial course. It can be up to 5 km long (but rarely is) and should be completed

PTV – The step up.

within an optimum time, calculated at roughly 12 km/h depending on type of terrain, length of course, etc. A number of obstacles (normally sixteen) occurs around the course, designed to test the competitor's ability to deal with the type of hazard that might be encountered during a hack or trail ride. Up to ten points can be awarded for effectiveness and style at each obstacle, with the sum of points from all phases determining the final placings of the event. It is not unusual for prizes to be awarded in each phase, as well as for overall performance.

CHAPTER TWO

Basic Skills

IN THIS SECTION WE LOOK AT THE BASIC SKILLS required for competition, and in particular we look at three key areas: riding skills, orienteering skills and attitude.

It has already been intimated that the competition requires a broad range of skills, and these basic skills should be developed to the highest degree possible by the individual. However, it must be stressed that this does not require the individual to be incredibly fit, to spend hours in solitary training or to be highly competitive. These things can contribute to an individual's personal enjoyment of the competition but one of the great things about TREC is that you can enjoy events without these things being highly developed, and the gulf between these two types of competitor is not a gaping chasm that cannot be bridged.

Looking at attitude first, competitors tend to measure the competition against their own last performance or against the individual who set the course rather than the other riders, so the sense of satisfaction and achievement can be as keenly felt at any level. It is also why there is considerable degree of help and encouragement between competitors, who share a close camaraderie.

The whole question of attitude is one that needs to be carefully considered, and each individual should recognise their particular motivating factor(s). Winning may never be the most important factor for many people. One of the most important shifts in attitude that needs to be made to get maximum enjoyment out of TREC is to adopt what can best be described as a 'can do' attitude. This is not something that needs the services of a sports psychologist, but a recognition and acceptance that what we are asking of ourselves, and our horses, is actually pretty basic, and is

POR – 'It's the other way, boys!'

well within all our capabilities.

Perhaps the secret of being successful and enjoying the event is to combine this positive 'can do' approach, with an open, flexible attitude of mind. Plan to enjoy the event too. There is little point in climbing onto a horse's back if you are not expecting to enjoy the experience. The horse senses this, and a happy, relaxed, and positive rider stands a much better chance of getting a good response from the horse than one that is feeling apprehensive and generally miserable about the whole prospect of competing.

With regard to riding skills, TREC does not ask you to ride in a way that is different from any other discipline, or from that which your instructor or coach tries to get you to aspire. All the skills are 'normal', and you will employ them to encourage your horse to do things that are well within its abilities (even if these things may seem a bit strange at first). Equally the tests set at each level are progressive, and should serve to stimulate the natural development of an effective leg and sympathetic hands. A balanced and relaxed body position will enable both you and your horse to cope with longer hours in the saddle.

Some new skills may be honed beyond what is required in your riding at present. As ever, getting the horse increasingly responsive to the leg is vital. The horse becomes more manoeuvrable and, with a firm leg giving it support, is less likely to panic in unusual situations. You will certainly want to rely less on the hand during the POR, as one hand tends to be well employed with a map and compass!

Riding sympathetically is something all riders strive to achieve, but when riding long distances this becomes very important. Any conflict, physical or mental, within the partnership can result in both getting exhausted for no good reason. Equally, developing the ability to read your horse, particularly its mental and physical state, and adjusting your reactions accordingly is vital. This can partly be learned from books and instructors, but there is nothing that can replace long hours spent in your horse's company intelligently observing its reactions and physical well-being.

Perhaps the biggest concern of new TREC converts is the map-reading or orienteering phase. Two key things for you to bear in mind when approaching a competition – no POR course designer (known as a *traceur*) is trying to get you hopelessly lost. It will make you angry and disillusioned as a competitor, and cause all sorts of headaches for the organisers if they have to find you. The *traceur* is trying to challenge you, and help you to develop map-reading skills at a level appropriate to the event. The other thing to bear in mind is that the *traceur* is not going to send you into places where it wouldn't be usual or normal for people to ride, so if you find yourself faced with a cliff to climb or impenetrable undergrowth, double check the map!

Equally, the standard of skills expected of you, particularly in the early levels of competition, are not excessive. They involve making basic decisions about interpreting what you see on the map and matching that information to what you see around you. This will enable you to make the right choice about which way to turn at a junction, or which track to take through the woods, always bearing in mind that the competition is a test of basic route finding abilities.

Map-reading is not some mystical art that you were either born able to do or not. And certainly, it is not something that one gender is good at, and the other is not. There appears to be adequate scientific evidence to demonstrate that the way in which males and females view maps and interpret the information may differ, but map-reading is a skill that can be learnt by anybody.

Although you will find some training advice about map-reading, this book does not have the scope to cover this fully. This can be done through reading books specifically on navigation, attending training classes (many people outside the equestrian world are expert navigators and can help with mastering the basics), and even by having a go at foot orienteering under the guidance of the British Orienteering Federation. Their competitions are carefully graduated according to difficulty and it is perfectly possible to enjoy one of these events without being a super-fit athlete. There are many classes where it would not be unusual to turn up in your wellies with the dog, and stroll around practising your skills. For more information look on their website http://www.britishorienteering.org.uk. You can find details of events and their levels, and there are even classes where you can follow a route marked with string just to give you an idea of how the ground compares with the map.

Without doubt, the vital thing to practise at home before you enter an event is to get used to carrying a map while riding. It will help you start to match features and symbols from the map to those things that are familiar around you, without the concern of getting lost in a strange place. You will start to develop an appreciation of matching distances on the map to real distances as you ride along, and with this practice comes confidence, so that maps no longer are alien artifacts to be shunned and feared. You will probably learn lots of things from the map that you didn't know about the places where you regularly ride too.

It will help you enormously if, by the time you enter your first few competitions, you understand that the map is a bird's eye view of the ground drawn to scale; that it is easier to follow a route on a map if you always hold the map so that features and directions on the map correspond to those on the ground (known as setting or orientating the map); that the top of the map corresponds with North; you know what a grid reference is; and you know how to use a compass. These are all simple skills that can be acquired in a day, and then developed with practice.

TRAINING AND PREPARATION

With regard to your individual training and preparation, you are the best person to judge what your weaknesses are, and which areas need most work. Very many people successfully enter their first TREC events without giving a great deal of thought to preparation, and this is certainly one way of identifying your own weak areas. Don't be put off from just having a go, as the officials, judges and other competitors will all be eager to see you enjoy your first event and will offer help.

However, you may like to be just a small step ahead and there are a number of things that you can do to make your first event a more relaxed and enjoyable venture.

Take every opportunity to learn about maps. As suggested previously, one of the very practical ways of doing this is to ride with a map at home. It helps to get you used to simply holding the map and looking at it, judging distances, getting familiar with symbols, and with orientating the map as you change direction (put very simply, the top of any printed Ordnance Survey map is always North, so, by using your compass and turning the map in your hand as you turn, always keep the top of the map pointing in the same direction as the North directional arrow on your compass and you will keep the map matching the ground around you). This will make decisions about which way to turn much easier, and enable you to recognise just where you are more quickly.

You don't have to be riding to do this. You can practise these simple techniques when out walking the dog, or even as a passenger in a car if you have the right map to work with. The more familiar and comfortable you are with a map, the more relaxed you will be when you come to compete.

We should say a brief word about map scales before we move on. A map is a vertical plan of a particular area drawn to scale. This scale is normally expressed as a ratio, e.g. 1:25,000. This means that one unit on the map equals 25,000 of those units on the ground. So looking at the 1:25,000 maps that are most often used in TREC events, one centimetre on the map equals 25,000 centimetres on the ground, or 250 m. Each grid square on our Ordnance Survey maps measures 4 cm across, so the distance on the ground across the area covered by a grid square is 1km, and across the diagonal of the grid square, about 1.5km.

This can help you gauge approximate distances quickly and, as you will see from the relevant section under POR, this will help you come up with a system for judging your speed accurately from the map.

Thousands of books have been written about training horses generally, and nearly all of them have some relevance to TREC as the sport is about using your horse in an entirely normal way. Certainly, for the POR phase you do want to have your horse relaxed and forward going. Map-reading can be a very difficult exercise on an excited horse. Equally, you will be much better off if both you and your horse do everything with the minimum of fuss and effort, thereby conserving energy. Your horse should be used to being ridden on a fairly loose rein, moving forward and changing direction relying on the leg and shifts in weight.

It can be a source of enormous frustration if your horse will not stand still while you examine your map, perhaps as you take a bearing off the map, or generally just work out where you are. It is not just on the PTV where it is important that your horse stands still while you mount too. It is highly likely that you will get on and off your horse a number of times during a POR, whether to deal with a problem, take a break at a checkpoint or to help the horse on very steep going. So training your horse to stand still can be an enormous benefit to you.

With regard to fitness training for your horse, this depends very much on the level of competition that you are entering. As with most equestrian disciplines, the fitter you and your horse are within reason, the easier life can be. However, you are not entering the Olympic marathon and, for a Level 1 event, your horse is going for a two-hour hack with a bit of cantering on the PTV. If you regularly hack your horse more than a couple of times a week, with perhaps one longer ride of more than two hours' duration each week, you and your horse will be more than adequately fit to tackle a Level 1 or even a Level 2 competition.

For the Control of Paces, the focus in your preparation should be on good old-fashioned flatwork or dressage, developing relaxed obedience to the aids, balance throughout all the paces, and an acceptance of an effective leg. This work pays dividends in everything that you do with your horse, and there is nothing that can replace time spent with an instructor or coach, working on the basic classical riding skills. Not only will this improve your performance on the Control of Paces, it will improve every aspect of your competitive performance in every phase of the event.

In the canter, you are aiming for a degree of collection to enable you comfortably to score maximum points, and this will also make the possibility of ten points on the bending poles a realistic target. The greatest benefit can be had from getting your horse to canter past unusual objects calmly. Concentrate on keeping the horse relaxed and straight, maintaining a constant rhythm on the approach and as you pass the object, with plenty of support from the lower leg. Again, the PTV will benefit from this sort of exercise as well as the Control of Paces.

The walk is a much more difficult pace to 'school'. Classical schooling philosophy discourages interfering with a horse's natural walk, but there are still a few things that we can work on. Making sure your horse develops a relaxed walk, which you can reproduce in competition, is a great first step. If this walk can be on a 'long rein', so much the better. A longer, lower outline enables the horse to take longer strides, so while the walk rhythm remains the same you are actually covering the ground more quickly.

Another technique that you can employ is to take advantage of your horse's own personality. The vast majority of riders when questioned agree that their own horse generally speeds up when returning from a hack over the last half kilometre, as they anticipate the pleasure of returning to the stable/field, a small feed perhaps and the prospect of relaxing after work.

Initially, when your horse's walk speeds up while heading home, do something yourself that the horse can sense that is unique to that situation. Some riders might gently tap the neck in rhythm with the walk, or make a slight sound such as whistling in time with the walk. Done every time when returning to the stables, the horse will start to associate the faster walk with whatever you are doing. Once this repetitive process has firmly established a link in your horse's mind, you can use whatever you have chosen as your 'trigger' to provoke the fast walk response. Essentially, you are looking to exploit a Pavlovian response in your horse.

The final phase (normally) is the PTV.

Every course at every competition will be different, and this is not just because of the terrain. Each organiser can choose from a number of obstacles and can put them in any order to make up the sixteen normally found on a PTV course. The aim of this phase is to test that you and your horse can negotiate an area of countryside, ideally of mixed terrain, and successfully deal with a number of obstacles that it would not be unreasonable for you to be faced with while out on a long hack or trail ride.

Essentially, the obstacles either are, or simulate, things that you would deal happily with if you encountered them outside a competition. This is one of the reasons that the jumping obstacles are not big (just under 1 m is the maximum height in a World Championships), and you would probably not encounter more than three jumps on any one course. The PTV should certainly not be viewed as a jumping course, and in a way the jumps tend to be the easier aspects of any course.

Getting around any PTV course is a comparatively straightforward thing. Doing it well can be quite a different matter, and that is just the point. The PTV is not meant as an extreme test of athletic performance at any level, but at every level it will present you with things that challenge all your basic riding skills, and the degree of aptitude your horse has as a saddle horse. This latter concept is something that we have lost sight of to an extent in Great Britain. Our breeding programmes are chiefly driven by the desire to produce the ultimate performance horse in any particular discipline, and it is to other countries that we look to see them developing breeding programmes aimed at producing excellent 'riding' horses.

Although Britain possibly has the largest market in the world for leisure riding in proportion to its population, little effort is put into breeding horses for this market. This is not to say that there are not a huge

PTV – Even a big horse, when properly schooled, can make the S-bend seem easy.

number of excellent saddle horses in the country, but they have appeared by an accident of breeding rather than according to any planned programme.

The PTV will test your horse as a saddle horse, in a wide variety of ways. It will test that your horse can safely cross varied terrain but not with the emphasis on speed, and that it can cope with dealing with a wide range of tests that challenge it physically and mentally. It is here where the real challenge of the PTV lies. Each obstacle encountered poses a dramatically different challenge from the one that went before and the one that is to follow, and it is your horse's ability to deal with these fast-changing demands that will determine success.

Equally, you are going to be challenged in the same way, having to adapt quickly from a jumping test to something that wouldn't be too out of place in the dressage arena. But never lose sight of the fact that these tests are exactly what horse and rider have been demonstrating excellence in for thousands of years – the ability to operate together as an intelligent partnership at a basic level of all round performance.

So your preparation for the PTV phase, apart from an appropriate degree of fittening work, should focus on getting your horse relaxed and responsive in unusual situations. When hacking at home, look for unusual situations to which you can safely introduce your horse, so that it gets used to new experiences. The day everyone puts their dustbins and bin bags out is a great day to go for a hack! Seek out terrain that is varied to get your horse accustomed to riding over ground that is not flat and smooth. You will be amazed at how steep a gradient your horse can climb and descend.

Try not to get into a complete and unchanging routine about your hacking at home. Avoid the 'we always have a canter here' syndrome, or 'we always go this side of the tree' pattern. Choose to do things differently as a matter of routine, if that isn't too much of a contradiction in terms.

Encouraging your horse constantly to venture just beyond its comfort zone will develop a growing confidence as he discovers that he can deal with new situations. With many of these instances, if you are working on one specific area of improvement, it can help enormously to have an assistant on the ground. Look for small improvements each time rather than one huge solution to a problem. There are times when that may happen, but you need to beware of getting yourself into a direct conflict with your horse, particularly a conflict that you cannot come out of ahead. Even to win a single huge battle may not be a good solution for you, as your horse may remember the trauma of whatever you were trying to do, and while being obedient in the future may never be completely confident and relaxed about it. This will result in a poorer performance.

Far better to avoid a major 'situation', and aim to achieve small improvements each and every time that you ride. As you would in other equestrian disciplines, make your training progressive. No one would introduce a young horse to show jumping by asking it to jump a 4-foot oxer, or to flatwork by asking for *piaffe*. So you too must make your PTV training progressive.

These small achievements which can be accomplished as part of your routine riding will make your first BHS TREC competition so much easier and more enjoyable.

PART TWO

THE COMPETITION

CHAPTER THREE

Equipment

OFTEN THE FIRST FORMAL PART of a competition may be an equipment check prior to anyone venturing out on the POR. This check is intended to ensure that you have a basic level of equipment to help you complete this phase of the competition, and the compulsory list (consult the current *BHS TREC Rulebook – see Appendix 3*) should be viewed as the minimum required to enable you to complete a trail ride successfully. As experience is gained, you will add particular items to this compulsory list that suit you.

Broadly speaking, the check looks at the serviceability of your tack, that you are equipped to deal with basic navigation, any simple injuries to you or your horse, and changes in the weather. It is also vital that you are equipped with appropriate safety wear, and visible information about your identity to be used in an emergency.

When planning what equipment to carry, strict attention should be paid to the amount of weight your horse will end up carrying, and the distribution of the weight load. Evenly distributed, a load should not discomfort your horse or alter its stride pattern, whereas slightly uneven loads can force your horse into taking shorter steps. So, when looking for equipment to suit your own needs, always look for light and durable items.

The equipment check itself can be quite a complicated and formal affair at a Championship event, with riders being asked to lay out all their equipment for inspection. However, at Level 1 and 2 events the inspection will probably be very brief and carried out as you are waiting to go in the map room. Normally, helmet standards will be physically checked but the rest of the inspection might only consist of a few questions. But do be warned, some officials like to put elements of the equipment check into

Facing page:
POR – Last-minute adjustments.

the POR phase itself, with different checkpoints checking for different items of equipment.

With regard to pairs, at Level 1 and 2 the pair might only have to carry the required equipment between them. However, most of the equipment has been identified as being useful to someone on a trail ride and the question that should occur to both members of a pair is, 'What happens should we get separated?' In the higher levels of competition, both members of the pair must be independently equipped.

Here are a couple of other general points about equipment. All the listed items have a purpose, so it should not just be a case of having them to satisfy the requirements of the competition. A compass is a compulsory item, but hidden away in an inside pocket it is not going to help you. Equally, a first-aid kit carried entirely on the horse is not going to help you if you have fallen off and your horse (and first-aid kit!) is disappearing into the distance.

Running through the equipment requirement, the following will help you approach your first competition with confidence.

The horse/pony – may compete unshod providing that it is normally kept that way. However, it must be stressed that you should be in a position to deal with a mixture of all types of terrain, and that can include tarmac roads or stony ground. Horses should be properly cared for and fit enough to cope with the level of event, but there is no expectation that the horse should be plaited or presented in a special way for any of the phases, other than properly groomed as a matter of routine welfare.

However, developing pride in your turnout can have a very beneficial effect on morale in general. Specifically, it is important to have a clean horse, as on long rides any dirt can provoke rubbing and cause sores. Do make sure that your horse has been groomed, particularly in areas where tack is fitted, and in places where dirt could cause rubbing during prolonged exercise. Horses generally feel better when they are clean and have been groomed, and a happier horse is going to perform better for you. The natural cooling mechanisms of a horse can also be impaired by a crust of dried sweat and/or mud, so keeping your horse clean is not just a visual thing.

TACK

Basic tack must remain the same throughout all phases, so saddles/bits/bridles should not be changed during an event. Tack should fit your horse correctly. If you have any doubts or concerns, seek advice from your instructor and consult a qualified saddle fitter. However, the choice of the type of tack is very flexible allowing for anything that is considered normal in the broad equestrian world. So Western tack, sidesaddles, bitless bridles etc. are all acceptable. The rules do forbid the use of standing martingales and other types of fixed reins.

Make sure that your tack is clean, as dirty tack wears out more quickly and can also cause rubbing to your horse. You should also regularly check all your tack to see that it is all serviceable, and there is nothing that needs repairing or replacing. It can be very annoying, not to say dangerous, to have something break during a competition. It is worth carrying a bare minimum of replacements in your POR kit. A few leather straps, a couple of clips or buckles and some string or baler twine should be sufficient.

POR – Working on the map at a checkpoint.

During the POR, you must carry a headcollar and lead rope so that the horse can be tied under suitable circumstances. Most riders put the headcollar on the horse with the lead rope tied around the horse's neck. However, it is perfectly acceptable to carry both elsewhere, and some competitors now use a combination headcollar/bridle with a lead rope. If tack includes a running martingale, a headcollar and lead rope will also be required on the PTV, as you must not lead from the reins with the running martingale attached when dismounted.

Many riders use saddlebags of some type for the POR, but these and their contents can be discarded for the other two phases. These are refinements, which are not immediately necessary when first tackling an event. You can carry most of the equipment for Levels 1 and 2 on your person, with the addition of a small 'bum-bag' or knapsack, and it is certainly recommended that when starting out you don't rush off and buy lots of equipment. Try the competition first, and make sure that you enjoy it before spending any money on extra equipment.

RIDER

You must wear a helmet to currently approved standards at all times while mounted. On your feet you should have footwear suitable for riding but again you are offered a fair degree of freedom. Most TREC competitors are not enthusiastic about traditional long boots (leather or rubber), and prefer ankle boots worn with half-chaps. It is worth bearing in mind that you might want to walk for a while on the POR to give your horse a rest, and long boots are not always the most comfortable things to walk in. Equally, on the PTV you may be hopping on and off your horse, and leading him up and down steep slopes, so a boot with a sole that has some grip is highly desirable.

Between head and foot, you are free to choose clothing that is suitable, practical and comfortable. There is no recognised uniform as such, so you can wear the clothes that you normally ride in. The things to consider for the POR phase are comfort (you may, depending on the level, be out on the course for six or seven hours), weight (as little as possible) and the weather (waterproofs are an essential item, but a number of layers of clothing gives you maximum flexibility to deal with changing weather conditions).

POR – A well-equipped rider. Note: most riders choose not to wear gloves, so it is easier for them to use their compass and map.

One additional word with regard to waterproofs. A reasonably good quality, lightweight jacket should be considered as the minimum, but you may want to take more depending on the time of year, weather forecast and the expected length of the course. It is all too easy to make map-reading mistakes when tired. If you are cold and wet too, then mistakes are almost inevitable. Plan to keep warm and comfortable throughout the POR phase, bearing in mind that this may mean putting on and taking off layers as the weather changes.

From 2004, the rules required you to wear fluorescent clothing on your torso during the POR. Ideally, this should be reflective too and is considered as a minimum. Additional hi-viz material on the helmet, and leg bands on the horse are encouraged. A fluorescent jacket or waistcoat worn outside will meet this requirement, but there are also now many examples of specialist competition bibs that will cover this rule, and enable you to carry the various items of equipment that you need to get at easily during the POR.

In 2005, it became compulsory for both horse and rider to carry identification tags. Not yet the full medical armbands, these tags should give the name of horse and rider, the competitor's competition number and the competition's emergency phone number. You can see from this that you will need to change some of this information at each and every competition. This information should be easily visible on both horse and rider, and it does need to be on both, in case the rider is separated from the horse at some point, particularly on the POR.

POR – You have time to read your map if your pony stands still.

Bibs aside, many riders wear cheap 'fisherman' type waistcoats. They have many pockets in which to carry small items of equipment, and can be left packed and ready all the time (they are ready to use on any trail ride, of course).

COMPULSORY ITEMS

- **Compass** – on person – do attach the compass to your body, as there is nothing worse than dropping a compass and having your trusty equine partner step on it! Many competitors carry a spare.

- **Pens** – these are vital and are not normally supplied. A pen with a narrow nib and bright colour is recommended for the map. Orange Pentel Hybrid Gel Markers are very popular for marking the map as they don't clash with colours used when making the map, and they are clearly visible but don't obscure what is underneath. A pen or pencil for making notes or marking distances on the map is also useful.

- **First-aid kit** – a couple of bandages, some antiseptic wash and some sterile dressings will meet the requirements but individuals may want to carry more. Certainly carry the bulk of this on the horse, but a few plasters, a bandage and a couple of sterile dressings on your person is always a good idea.

POR – Some of the equipment.

- **Torch** – a small hand-held torch will get you through the equipment check. Make sure the batteries work, and carry spares. However, if you were caught out as it got dark would you be happy relying on this? Most regular competitors carry a reasonably powerful head torch stowed in their saddlebags.

- **Whistle** – to signal for help in an emergency.

- **Emergency farriers' tools** (suitable for the removal of a shoe) and a protective boot (Level 3 and above).

A few words about the rules relating to farriers' tools and a protective boot. While you are not required to carry this equipment at Level 1 and 2, you would still be prevented from leaving a checkpoint on the POR if you had lost a shoe and were unable to make some provision to protect your horse's hoof. There are certainly examples of riders competing at Level 1 or 2, who in an effort to save weight have not carried this equipment, lost a shoe on the POR, and consequently had to abandon their hopes of doing well.

It also must be stressed that any farriers' tools carried can only be used to remove a loose shoe so a protective boot can be fitted. Any other work that needs to be done on your horse's feet must be left to those qualified to do so.

OTHER RECOMMENDED ITEMS

- **Map case** – you must be able to keep your map dry if it rains. There are many types of map case available. Some people prefer the larger type, which they can fold, some prefer a smaller one as being less cumbersome, and some prefer ones that you can see into from either side. Find one that suits you but whichever you choose, the vital thing is that your map case keeps the maps dry and that it is attached to you. Some competitors insert a piece of stiff board into the map case to make writing on the map easier during the POR.

- **Digital watch or stopwatch** – you will need this to help maintain your speeds on the POR. Most digital watches include a stopwatch so you needn't have to have two separate items. Again, this is something that can break, or the batteries run out right in the middle of a competition, so many regular competitors carry a spare. You may also see some competitors sporting very sophisticated devices on their wrists. These days, you can get watches that include a stopwatch, compass, barometer, altimeter – everything but a microwave to cook your lunch for you! These can be very useful but are certainly not necessary when first starting out.

• **Money** – always useful to have some cash on you.

• **Mobile phone** – for use in an emergency.

• **Refreshments** – some events will give you a packed lunch but don't rely on this. They also tend to be bulky, so many riders prefer to carry the things they know they like and that keep them going. Many chemists offer hydrating drinks in collapsible cartons, and many outdoor pursuits or mountain-biking shops sell high energy/high carbohydrate flavoured gels in collapsible cartons. Again, don't get carried away – a bottle of water and a bar of chocolate will get most people happily through a Level 1 event. But whatever you carry, make sure you take your rubbish home with you.

• **Penknife** – a penknife can come in handy in all sorts of situations, and there are now many examples of excellent 'multitools' on the market, which offer a great deal more than the traditional penknife. Be warned though, some of the cheaper ones are just not robust enough.

There are some other items that you may want to carry, particularly during the POR, but these are covered in the section concerning the POR.

You will find an equipment checklist in Appendix 3.

You can wear spurs and carry a whip during any of the phases if you want to. There is no requirement to wear a body protector during any of the phases but if you wish to, you certainly can and it is recommended that you wear one to current EU standards if you do.

CHAPTER FOUR

Phase 1 (POR) – Orienteering

Parcours d'Orientation et de Regularité

THIS PHASE IS IMMENSELY POPULAR with competitors and for many it is the reason that they do TREC. Depending on the level of the event, it is during the POR when riders are able to spend the maximum amount of time with their horses – anything from two hours in a short event, up to seven or eight hours in a Championship.

For a pair, they must enjoy each others' company and be able to suppress annoyance about mistakes made by the other person. An individual must enjoy the solitude and be happy relying on his or her own resourcefulness.

The two elements of the POR test are firstly to follow a given route on a map accurately, and secondly to cover the distance between the various checkpoints as close to the required speed as is possible.

The organisers of an event decide on a route for the event, after having explored the area that they are intending to use for this phase. While it may be possible to plan a route in outline from a map, at some point the route must be physically examined by the person who will draw the route onto the master maps that will be used in the map room. This is done to determine that there are no mistakes on the map itself, that the route is safe, that there are no physical barriers to horses such as locked gates, and to site the various checkpoints at appropriate points on the route.

As previously stated, the person who does this is known as the *traceur* (in many competitions this may well be the TD), and they have an extremely difficult job. With the organiser, they are trying to give all the competitors a really pleasant route, which the riders will enjoy even if they don't get all the navigation correct. It is worth reiterating that it is the *traceur's* intention to test the competitors' navigational skills according to the level of competition but not to get people hopelessly lost. If this happens, it is an administrative headache for the organisers and an unpleasant and demoralising experience for the riders. Getting the balance of difficulty correct is a taxing job.

It is also an aim of the *traceur* not to trick competitors with the problems that he or she sets them. This sounds simple but can be difficult to achieve. Parts of any route will be straightforward and parts will be technically demanding, and it is not necessarily obvious from looking at the map which is which. With experience, riders do develop an extra sense, which helps them spot areas of likely difficulty in the map room, especially if they are familiar with the *traceur* from previous competitions. The *traceur* wants to test the competitors' skills but in a way that is logical for someone on a journey. Although it does happen, *traceurs* try to avoid setting a test that, perhaps because of a difference between the map and the ground, appears to the rider as a trick rather than a logical and precise test of navigational skills.

PROCEDURES

When you first enter a competition, you will be sent a series of start times relating to the various phases of the event. With a one-day competition, it is not unusual for the Control of Paces and PTV phases to be run before the POR. However, for a two-day competition, except in exceptional circumstances, the POR will come first, so we shall start there.

For POR start times it is usual to receive three times – an inspection or equipment check time, a map room time and a departure time. The information would look something like this:

rider no.	name	equip. check	map room	depart
1	A. Somebody	10.00 am	10.05 am	10.15 am

Normally, you would be expected to appear with your horse at a designated place (almost certainly adjacent to the map room), ready to depart on the POR just before your allotted time for the equipment check. Five minutes is normally sufficient for the equipment check. The official will ask to see probably five items from the list of mandatory equipment. These five items will vary from event to event. Occasionally, there may be a further check on some of these items at a checkpoint during the POR.

Obviously, it is not expected that anyone would discard any items of compulsory equipment after this check before setting off. Quite apart from the rules, there are very good reasons why it is desirable to have this equipment with you on a trail ride.

Following your equipment check, you will be required to wait until called into the map room. Use this time to make sure that you are carrying everything that you will need in the map room and that it is all easily accessible. You don't want to be wasting precious time in the map room trying to locate your reading glasses! Also, check that your horse is ready to go when you exit the map room.

You should be prepared to tie your horse up while in the map room. The event organiser will have made some provision for waiting horses but this will vary from event to event. If you know your horse will not tie up (and do aim to train it at home to do this), you should make yourself responsible for finding a friend to hold your horse for you while you are in the map room.

There are other very useful things that you can do while waiting outside the map room. Often the official time is displayed outside the map room, so you will have a chance to adjust your watch to the official time. (The significance of official time will be explained when we get onto the scoring for this phase.) At this point, you still will not have a map, as this is supplied to you by the organiser in the map room. However, look around and try to imagine how the immediate area would be represented on a map. Get your compass out and work out which way is North, so that you have an idea which directions (North, South, East etc.) the obvious departure routes away from the map room run. Naturally, you will also watch competitors ahead of you leaving to get clues from the direction in which they set off. Don't assume too much from watching just one. They may have got it wrong. Equally, there may be a number of different routes being used to get competitors away from the map room.

However, being able to picture in your mind the path that you will take to leave, as soon as you sit down in the map room can be a great confidence boost. Most competitors want to get away from the map room as quickly as possible. Nobody wants to come out of the map room and be seen by others to dither. Even if you can only get out of sight around the first corner, and then have to stop to get yourself organised, fold your map up into its map case, and work out where to go now.

You should be called into the map room just in advance of your allotted time, but keep an eye on the watch and hover. You want to make sure that you are sitting down in the appropriate place ready to start marking

POR – A pair working on their maps. Their horses can be seen waiting in the background.

the map at your start time, unless the organisers have told you that there is a delay. Whatever time has been allocated to you for map marking (normally 10, 15 or 20 minutes depending on the level) you want to spend every minute of that time marking your map.

When you sit down you should have in front of you a master map (often stuck to the table so that no competitor can accidentally leave with it) with the route marked on it (see illustration below), a map sheet that covers the same area but without a route marked on it (which becomes your map) and a record card. This is your own record card, which you must carry during the POR phase on which the officials record the times that you arrive and leave checkpoints. It is an important document for you, as it should mirror the information recorded by the officials at checkpoints, so do not lose it or allow it to get wet and unusable. When officials write information on the card, check it, as it is your way of checking that the information that they are recording is correct. You may not agree with the time that they have

POR – The route leaving the start.

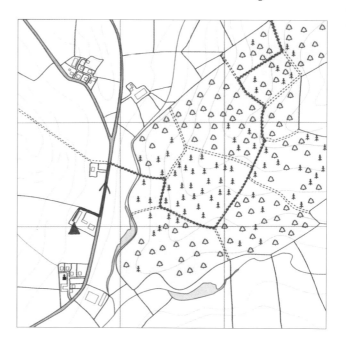

given you – a quick check may show that they have misread their watch or just written something down incorrectly. This may not be solved immediately at a checkpoint, but at least you have registered it as a problem and you can ask to have that fact recorded.

It is worth stressing at this point that all the officials are doing their best to get everything right, and are trying very hard to avoid mistakes. Mistakes do happen, but it does not help solve problems to get angry and aggressive with the officials. They may not even be able to rectify a mistake until the technical delegate is consulted. If you are faced with such a problem, ask to have it recorded and then forget it. Being angry about something that has already occurred will have a detrimental effect on the rest of your performance.

This is also true if you make a genuine mistake. Having made a mistake, forget it. Don't let it prey on your mind so that you don't concentrate fully on getting everything else right. It is highly likely that many other people will have made the same or a similar mistake to you, so don't worry about it. It is in the past – focus on getting the future right.

Also displayed somewhere in the map room will be the speed that you are required to travel at from the map room to the first checkpoint that you reach. It will be in kilometres per hour (km/h) and can vary between 6 km/h and 12 km/h, so it may be that your start speed might be 7.3 km/h. Although the map room official will point this out to you, it is your responsibility, not the officials, to ensure that you do not leave the map room without knowing this speed. In exceptional circumstances, this speed might be below 6 km/h (if the terrain over the first stage is very rough or steep) but at no point during a POR phase in any competition will you be given a speed above 12 km/h.

There are a few other general things to bear in mind at the start. The map room is usually designated as Checkpoint 1, so don't panic when the first checkpoint that you reach turns out to be Checkpoint 2. You haven't missed a checkpoint already! You also will only know the location of Checkpoint 1 (the map room) in advance. The location of all the other checkpoints are unknown to you until you arrive at them. This is very significant when it comes to judging speed, which is why there is a major section about the methods for judging speed during competition in this book.

In the map room, accurately recording the official route on to your own map sheet is clearly vital, as you can't hope to ride the correct route if it isn't marked on your map sheet correctly in the first place. It can be useful to have a magnifying glass in your equipment to check complicated bits on the master map, so the first thing that you might do after locating the start (where you are), which is normally marked with a red triangle, is quickly to scan the whole route. With competition experience, many competitors will immediately get a sense of where the difficult parts of the route are, and where checkpoints might be sited. They may even have a system for marking these points on the map as a reminder, such as simply putting an exclamation mark next to the bit of the route that makes them immediately suspicious.

When competitors and *traceurs* get to know each others' abilities and attitudes very well, an interesting intellectual war can develop, with the competitor familiar with the *traceur's* normal thinking about routes and his/her favourite types of test, while the *traceur* is constantly thinking of how to avoid being predictable.

Having scanned the route, start to mark your map. Each competitor has a preferred way of doing this, but one very useful method is to mark short sections backwards. Pick a very identifiable point on the route (probably a junction or clear change in terrain) about 2 cm from the start and mark the route back to the start. If for some reason your route does not come back to the start precisely, then you have probably made a mistake. Keep leap-frogging ahead on the route, and mark backwards, so that you can use the method to check that you are accurate. It is by no means foolproof but is one of many ways of checking your accuracy.

One method that can save you a little time is to not mark the route where you are certain that you know where it goes. This may sound like a complete contradiction alongside all the other statements about the route being completely unknown to you. However, there will be parts of the route in nearly every competition you do, where you have to ride along a road (usually because there is no alternative). This may be for a number of kilometres. Where this happens, there is no real need to draw a line on your map. Just put an arrow pointing up the road in the direction that you should be traveling, and start again with an arrow pointing in the appropriate direction just before the end of the road section.

Continue until the whole route is marked, and aim to do this leaving sufficient time to go quickly over the whole route on both maps comparing them. Hopefully, you now have the tools to achieve one part of the POR test successfully, to follow the set route accurately from a map.

The second part of the POR test involves riding the stages between the checkpoints at the required or set speed. As you are already aware, you do not know where the checkpoints (your destinations over each stage) are, so you do not know the total distances you must travel at a particular speed and therefore cannot calculate the time that you must arrive at a checkpoint. If you are setting off on a motorway journey and you know that your intended destination is 120 miles away, and you are told to average 60mph, you know that you must take two hours to reach your destination. With the speedometer in a car, this is easily achieved (unless you are going around the M25).

However, in TREC you do not have a speedometer fitted to your horse, and indeed you do not know how far away your destination is, so you need to be able to control your speed from minute to minute as you ride, so that you can avoid arriving early or late at each checkpoint. There are a number of different ways of doing this, and you may find that one suits you better than another. It is possible that your preferred method for doing this is not a practical option if, for instance, it is raining heavily, so mastering more than one of these methods of controlling your speed may be necessary.

Before continuing, it is worth considering the natural speed of your horse in each of its paces. An initial mistake that many doing TREC for the first time make is to think that they control their speed throughout the POR by knowing how fast their horse walks, trots and canters. While there are a number of reasons why this information is useful, as a means of gauging your overall progress it is not practical to rely on the knowledge of your horse's speed through its paces.

If you know that your horse walks at 6.9 km/h, trots at 8.1 km/h and canters at 10.5 km/h that is excellent, providing that you are only ever given those speeds. It becomes a mathematical nightmare to calculate how much walking and trotting you must do to stick to a speed of 7.6 km/h, and to take into account stopping for 56 seconds to cross a road, taking 75 seconds to open and shut a gate, halting for 105 seconds to work out which way to go, and riding in the wrong direction for 2½ minutes. So, as you will see shortly, we have to use artificial ways of calculating speed.

However, knowledge of your own horse's speeds throughout its paces is by no means useless information. It is a great aid for you to get an overall feel for how you are progressing. It also is a great aid to help you determine your route over short distances.

If you know that the turning that you are looking for in the forest is 250 m from where you enter the forest, and that your horse walks at 6 km/h you can be fairly certain that the turning that you reach in one minute is not the correct one. 250 m at 6 km/h should take you 2 minutes and 30 seconds.

This technique becomes vital in higher level competitions when competitors have their maps removed and are given only bearings and distances to navigate by. It is also a technique that can become vital at any level of competition, or even during a hack in a strange place if for some reason (fog perhaps) visibility is greatly reduced. Even to be in a familiar place and suddenly lose all visibility is a very frightening and intimidating thing to happen to anybody. However, to be equipped with a compass and the knowledge of how to use it, and to have a technique for physically judging distance, can turn this potentially frightening experience into just another simple piece of navigation.

When determining your horse's speed in each of its paces, you should be aware that its level of fitness will alter its speed, as will the type of terrain being covered, the amount of load that it is carrying and even how that load is distributed. British soldiers working with the Arabs in the Middle East during the First World War were never able to match the Arabs' skills in loading both horses and camels, and consequently could never keep up with them.

So when investigating your horse's relative speeds, be equipped as you would in a competition with a full load distributed as you would normally carry it. Remember also to ride him as you would in a competition. It is no good timing the horse in practice at the canter, riding as though you were doing the Control of Paces, when during an actual POR you would be riding on a much longer rein and allowing your horse to obtain a faster speed.

To determine your horse's speeds, select a suitable area of ground and then measure and mark out 100 m. You can refine this by recording speeds over rougher terrain, uphill, downhill, and so on, in due course to suit your own requirements. To do this properly, you really need at least one assistant to help you with the timing.

Simply time the walk, trot and canter over the 100 m. It is best to do this a number of times in each pace and take an average. It is also extremely useful if you do the same counting the number of strides your horse takes to cover the distance in each pace. You may find counting strides works better for you in competition than timing short sections. Equally, you may use the counting method as a double check on your timing. Record all this information on a piece of paper and laminate it, so that you have it to refer to in all weathers.

We will look at the two basic methods for determining speeds, which should give you a sound foundation on which you may well base personal variations that you find work best for you. Fundamentally, as is so often the case with anything to do with horses, there is no single and absolute right way to do this, so don't be afraid of experimenting to find the most suitable.

At the root of this lies the need to 'way-mark' the route to give you points of reference by which to judge your progress and speed. This is no different from many other equestrian disciplines that involve controlling speed. It is excellent to develop an instinctive knowledge of how fast you are going, and this 'seat of your pants' judgement can serve you perfectly well in getting things nearly right and giving you an idea of how much pressure you are putting on your mount physically. Eventers can spend many hours working on this ability to judge that they are travelling at a specific speed across country. But they would still not rely on this exclusively. They would also have walked the cross-country course a number of times with a measuring wheel, noting distinctive 'way-marks' that they must have reached by a certain time if they are to be traveling at the speed required to avoid time penalties.

You do not have the opportunity to way-mark your route on the ground, but you can way-mark the map in much the same way. By measuring the map, and marking on measured points of reference you will give yourself the ability to judge your speed, and there are two principal ways of doing this. Both can be done (or at least started in the map room), providing that you have some time left after marking the route.

The first method is to measure the route by distance, recording, at the least, half kilometre way-marks (a little pencil mark on the route every

POR – Quarter kilometre way-marks added to drawn route.

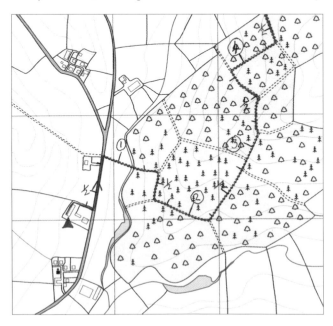

0.5 km). To give yourself a greater degree of accuracy, it is better to record every 250 m. See the map below left for example. You will also need a time/distance chart (see below) which shows you how long it should take you to cover 500 m at a particular speed.

You can use the following formula to find the time that it should take you at a particular speed to cover the distance that you want to know about. Take the distance and multiply it by 60. Divide that by the given speed, and that will give you the time it will take you to cover the original distance.

$$\frac{\text{distance x } 60}{\text{speed}} = \text{time taken}$$

So, if you are given a speed of 6 km/h, and you want to know how long it should take you to cover half a kilometre at that speed, you would mul-

Speed	Time to Travel Distance (metres)					
km/h	500	1,000	2,000	3,000	4,000	5,000
6	5 mins	10 mins	20 mins	30 mins	40 mins	50 mins
6.5	4.37	9.14	18.28	27.42	36.55	46.09
7	4.17	8.34	17.09	25.43	34.17	42.51
7.5	4	8	16	24	32	40
8	3.45	7.30	15	22.30	30	37.30
8.5	3.32	7.04	14.07	21.11	28.14	35.18
9	3.20	6.40	13.20	20.00	26.40	33.20
9.5	3.09	6.19	12.38	18.57	25.16	31.35
10	3	6	12	18	24	30
10.5	2.51	5.43	11.26	17.09	22.51	28.34
11	2.44	5.27	10.55	16.22	21.49	27.16
11.5	2.37	5.13	10.26	15.39	20.52	26.05
12	2.30	5	10	15	20	25

tiply 0.5 by 60 = 30. Divide by 6. The answer is 5, so it should take you five minutes to cover half a kilometre riding at 6 km/h. However, you really don't want to be doing such sums in a competition as you ride along. Far better to have a small laminated chart with you to use as a ready-reckoner. The easiest quick example of this for one speed would be:

Speed	6 km/h			
Distance	250 metres	500 metres	750 metres	1 km
Time	2 mins 30 secs	5 mins	7 mins 30 secs	10 mins

It is probably sufficient on this chart to list speeds at every ½ km/h starting at 6 km/h, up to 12 km/h as per the example, although you may be given speeds in between these (e.g. 8.2 km/h). To break your chart down to this degree can make it too cumbersome to use, and it is probably sufficient to guesstimate how long it should take you to cover 250 metres when you have each ½ km/h either side of the given speed as a point of reference. Perhaps at this point it is worth noting how the penalties work regarding speed.

Each competitor starts this phase with 240 points. Some can be lost during the equipment check (maximum ten points), but the majority can be lost by incurring penalties actually on the POR. We will come onto the penalties that can be incurred for navigating inaccurately shortly. With respect to the speed, one penalty point is earned by each whole minute the competitor is away (either too fast or too slow) from the official optimum time. This means that if the official time for a particular stage was 20 minutes, any competitor who took between 19 minutes, and 20 minutes 59 seconds would not incur any penalties. A competitor taking 18 minutes 59 seconds, or 21 minutes exactly would incur one penalty.

The official time is calculated by using a flat line measurement from the map. As no route can actually be flat in reality, it means that to cover the distance at a set speed of 6 km/h, for instance, the rider would have to be going faster than 6 km/h over the ground. However, as both the official distance and the rider's way-marking are done on the map, it makes no difference in practice.

So by looking at the map opposite, we can see that from the start at a speed of 8 km/h, meaning each 500 m should be covered in 3 minutes 45 seconds, a competitor should be at Point A in 3 minutes 45 seconds, Point B in 7 minutes 30 seconds, Point C in 11 minutes 15 seconds, etc. The competitor continues in this fashion until arriving at a checkpoint, where

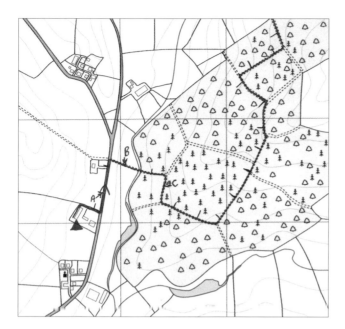

POR – After leaving the start, plan to be at A in 3 minutes 45 seconds, B in 7 minutes 30 seconds, C in 11 minutes 15 seconds, and continue to cover each half kilometre in 3 minutes 45 seconds until you reach the next checkpoint.

he or she will be given a new speed. The only difference between this next stage and the last is that it will take a different amount of time to cover each 250 m, as speeds always change at checkpoints. This is a very simple technique to use, the only slightly awkward thing to deal with is that checkpoints will very rarely fall conveniently on the measured mark, so a little mental juggling might need to be done to allow for the fact that you have only 105 m to travel from leaving a checkpoint to the next mark on your map.

You may want to take into account one other thing on your distance/time chart. You will never be given a speed greater than 12 km/h, but very occasionally you might get a speed below 6 km/h as mentioned previously. It would therefore be a good idea to have a separate chart for speeds below 6 km/h stored in your TREC equipment somewhere.

There are a number of ways of actually measuring the map and putting these distance way-marks on. You need to experiment a bit to find the one that works best for you. There is a wide variety of measuring devices available on the market, of which most are a form of measuring wheel. Some people (myself included) find them a bit clumsy to use, and consequently inaccurate. However, don't immediately write them off as some are certainly better than others, and it can always be the operator rather than the device that is clumsy!

Quite a number of competitors use a piece of string, which they have premarked with ¼, ½, ¾, 1 km etc. marks with which they overlay the

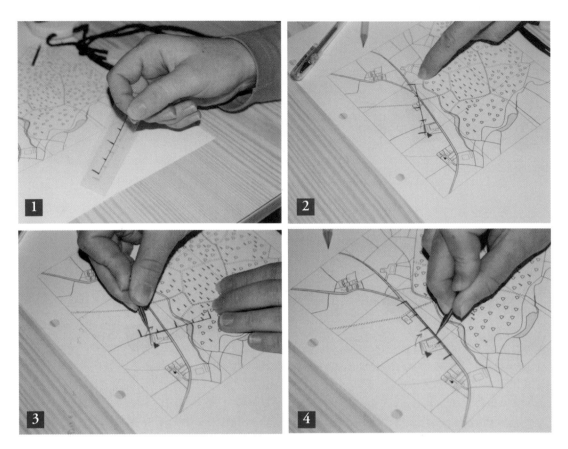

POR – Using a roamer to measure the route (see text).

route. They can then copy the distance marks off the string onto the map in the corresponding places.

Another very popular method is to use a 'roamer'. This is a home-made see-through ruler, which is normally flexible. Most are made out of the clear acetate that is used in the production of slides for overhead projectors. A rectangular piece is cut about 5 cm long and 1.5 cm wide. Using a ruler, mark down the centre of the acetate a line, using permanent ink, measuring 4 cm (which on a 1:25,000 map represents 1 kilometre), with the quarter, half-way and three-quarter points marked. This now becomes your ruler with which to measure the route.

The technique used is to overlay the route with one end of the measure over the point that you want to start measuring from on the map, and the line of the measure following the route marked on the map. At the first point where the marked route turns and diverges away from your measure, using a sharp point (this could be a horseshoe nail, pin or sharp pencil) as a fulcrum, the acetate is swivelled until the measure again superimposes the next bit of the route. You continue doing this, marking on the distance points, until the whole route (or as much as you have had time to mark) is covered.

So at this point, you are ready to leave the map room with the official route marked accurately onto your map, that route measured and a time/distance calculator to help you control your speed as you ride. One of the disadvantages of these methods is that you rarely have time to measure the whole route, so either you are going to have to continue to do this during a break at a checkpoint, or at some point your measured way-marks on the map are going to run out.

Some riders take a different approach to measuring the route with regard to controlling their speed. Evidence suggests that this method is probably the most efficient and accurate, but it comes with its own problems, one of which is explaining the concept clearly. Essentially, the route is measured in a very similar way to that described previously using a roamer, but with this method you are not going to measure distance but time. This method does away with the need for a time/distance calculator but requires a more complicated roamer, which while not impossible to make at home, is better machine produced.

The sort of roamer required is normally made out of clear perspex and is larger than the one described previously, measuring about 6 cm by 4 cm. Around the outside of the roamer are a number of different scales, normally starting at 6 and going up to 12 by half units. The scale at 6 will be half as long as the scale at 12. These different scales represent the distance that you should cover on a 1:25,000 map in 2½ minutes (distance covered in 5 minutes on a 1:50,000 map).

So, in a similar fashion, once the route is marked onto your map in the map room, you select the scale that corresponds as nearly as possible to the speed that you have been given for the first stage. For example, you

POR – Example of roamer used to measure time, instead of distance. The central grid is to help with grid references.

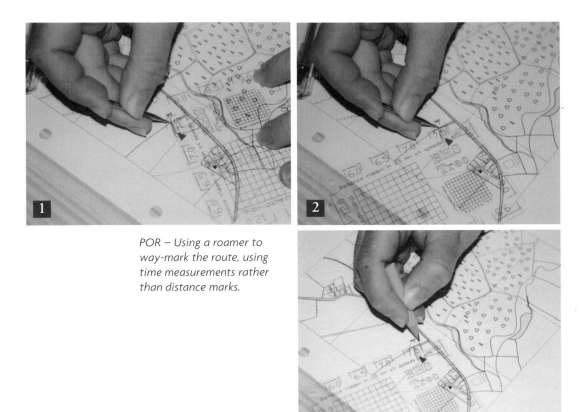

POR – Using a roamer to way-mark the route, using time measurements rather than distance marks.

are given 7.6 km/h as your starting speed, so you select the 7.5 scale on the edge of your roamer and use that to start measuring the route, remembering that each mark that you put on the map represents the distance that you must travel in 2½ minutes at that speed. You should therefore reach the first mark in 2½ mins, the second in 5 mins, the third in 7½ mins etc. So if you are delayed for some reason mounting and leaving the location of the map room, you know that you have to be pretty quick to reach the first marked point on your map within 2½ minutes. In reality, you would probably take a gamble and not aim to catch up all the lost ground by the first mark, but conserve your horse's energy a bit and be back on schedule by the second mark.

This method has a number of advantages. The first is that you are never trying to measure the whole map, because the scale that you use will change at every checkpoint. You hope to mark enough of the map to get you to the first checkpoint, so if we assume that this might take you 20 minutes you will only have had to put six marks on the map, something that can be done very quickly. How far you go can depend on a number of things. The speed that you are given – a stage with a faster speed tends to be shorter than one with a slower speed, the look of the terrain, and after a while you start to develop a sense of where checkpoints are likely to be. However this aside, it only takes a few moments to put another three or four marks on to your map especially if you have a piece of board in your map case which you can use as a miniature table (maybe your horse will stand still enough so that you can do it mounted!).

As soon as you are given a new speed at a checkpoint, you select the appropriate scale and repeat the process. So the second advantage means that mentally you never have to make an adjustment in time regarding the marks on your map. It should take you 2½ minutes to ride between each mark on the map – every time.

Obviously, you need to work on your map albeit briefly at every checkpoint. This gives you a great degree of flexibility, and overall saves you time. However, the need to work on the map at every checkpoint can also be this technique's downfall. If it is raining it becomes nearly impossible to work on the map once you have left the map room. There are any number of competitors who from bitter experience will tell you that maps fall apart very quickly if they get wet!

If you are drawn to this latter method, it is important to learn and practise the first method too, in case you ever end up competing in heavy rain.

This probably seems quite complicated and intimidating in a 'Beginner's Guide', but rather than be put off by this, you must remember that to get the speed a little wrong is hardly a disaster. Coming into a checkpoint from a wrong direction earns you 30 penalties. You would have to be 30 minutes late or early to pick up this many time penalties, so it is much better to concentrate on getting the route accurate than worrying a great deal about the speed.

You are now ready to leave the map room, when told to by the official in charge.

Once away from the map room, it is important to keep focused on the route. While every route should be enjoyable to ride, remember not to allow yourself to get sidetracked into looking at the scenery too much. Focus on getting the navigation correct, and then as a secondary issue the speed. Definitely 'less can be more' on the POR phase. By not concentrating too intently on the speed, but finding a rhythm that suits your navigational skills, less effort can produce more points.

Try to keep anticipating what should be ahead of you from the information on the map, so that you can use this to keep confirming to yourself that you are on the right route. Look ahead on the map to check for things that will help you confirm where you are. These might be a stream or drain running under the track that you are on, hedge lines or buildings off to the side of your route, particular shaped fields or hills/valleys that you ride past, or overhead power lines above you. You should be trying to use information from every available source around, above and below you – not just following the linear markings on your map.

When things don't quite make sense, stop immediately and assess what is the matter. Try to work out why things are not making sense, matching the map to the ground. If you cannot find an explanation, retrace your steps back to the point when things do start making sense again. Then begin the process, carefully examining each decision that you make paying particular attention to the distances that you travel between each 'point of decision'. When you are travelling along a straight route with no turnings there are really no decisions to make, other than to keep going. However, on every route there comes a moment when you decide that you must change direction, take a turning etc. These 'points of decision', once reached, form crisis points on your route. They are the points where you get things right or wrong. More often than not, mistakes are made by not estimating the distance between points of decision accurately enough.

The ability to do this accurately is not some strange mystic art or something that is in your genes. It can easily be acquired with practice. The closer together points of decision come, the more technical the navigation is, so a *traceur* for a Level 1 or 2 route would be trying to space out the points of decision. At the higher levels, the *traceur* will be forcing points of decision onto the competitor in quick succession. This is one of the reasons why this phase of TREC can be so exhausting mentally, once you are tackling longer routes.

Although this may sound like a contradiction, the key skill to acquire for long-term success is not to seek to be perfect. No one is a perfect navigator. However, the really good competitors are the ones who can rapidly assess whether they are on the right route as soon after a point of decision as possible, and correct a mistake if they have made one as quickly as possible. You learn from your mistakes, so in the quest to improve, don't be afraid of making them.

Providing you have made the right choice at your points of decision, you will arrive at the various checkpoints. And don't be intimidated at trying this. Hundreds upon hundreds of people who considered themselves totally hopeless and incompetent at map-reading have discovered that it is not impossible after all, and are fast becoming very successful TREC competitors as they progress through the levels.

When you arrive at a checkpoint, the judge will note the time that you arrive, and from which direction. The entrance to the checkpoint is indicated by small red and white flags (as per a cross-country fence) and they are there to be seen by the judge, not you. Indeed, you may not even notice them until after you have entered the checkpoint. The checkpoint judge may also indicate whether they consider that you changed gait on the way into the checkpoint. This can be a more contentious matter. The rules do not expect you to canter through the flags mowing down those already in the checkpoint, if you happen to have been cantering when you saw the checkpoint. The judge is really looking to see if, in his or her opinion, you have altered pace or gait after seeing the checkpoint in an attempt to alter the time that you arrive between the flags.

POR – A busy checkpoint in the woods, incorporating a vet check – and a chance for a breather!

These times are normally recorded as the horse's leading foreleg passes between the flags. In the case of a pair, times for arriving at, and leaving from checkpoints are determined by the last rider.

Ideally, checkpoints should be sited so that you come upon them unexpectedly and have next to no advance warning that you are arriving at a checkpoint. So if you were to trot around a corner to discover a checkpoint it would be quite normal for you to slow to a walk so that you entered the checkpoint in a safe and controlled manner. There should be no penalty for this.

However, it is not always possible to site a checkpoint in such ideal circumstances, so if it is possible for a competitor to view a checkpoint from a distance, and the judge considers that the competitor both saw the checkpoint and then did something to alter the time of arrival (either speeding up or slowing down) they may give you 30 penalties for 'changing gait'. The rules state that once seeing a checkpoint, you must come straight to that checkpoint by what you consider to be the correct route given to you.

Other penalties awarded can be 30 penalties for approaching a checkpoint from the wrong direction and one penalty for each full minute over or under the optimum time for the section. The judge can also award time penalties to people who do not leave the checkpoint at their appointed time of departure. Some people think that means that all they have to do is move outside the checkpoint, but in reality it is best to move out of sight of the checkpoint before stopping to deal with whatever needs to be dealt with.

If you miss a checkpoint, you earn yourself 50 penalties instantly. In addition, it is highly likely that you may also incur time penalties. These are calculated by adding the distances together from the last checkpoint that you did pass through to the next one that you reach. This total distance is applied to the speed that you were given on leaving your last checkpoint to determine the time that this should have taken you.

In addition to checkpoints, routes can have other methods of checking to see that you are on the correct route. These are generally known as tickets and can occur in a number of different forms. Some may be manned, but they can also be unmanned. In the case of the latter, there should be some indication before you set off (perhaps outside the map room) as to what an unmanned ticket would look like. The one thing that they all have in common is that you do not have an enforced stop at a ticket, and the speed would remain unchanged.

In terms of penalties, an error involving a ticket results in the same number of penalties as missing a checkpoint (50), but you need to be aware that there can be both good and bad tickets. A good ticket confirms that you are on the correct route, a bad ticket shows that you have taken an incorrect route. In designing a route, the *traceur* aims to ensure that a rider cannot be penalised twice by tickets for the same error in navigation (i.e. they miss a good ticket and find a bad ticket, logically earning 100 penalties, for making one mistake).

If a ticket point is manned you can also be penalised 30 points for arriving form the wrong direction.

You continue to make progress around the route given to you until you arrive at a checkpoint where the judge tells you that you have finished the

POR phase. This may not be where you expect it to be, and almost certainly it will be before you return to the venue. At this point, the POR is over and you will be instructed to return to the venue by the route shown on the map, or by another recommended route. This checkpoint may take your record card, or ask you to hand it in to a particular person/place on returning to the venue.

At this point, you can breathe a sigh of relief as you will have successfully completed the POR phase.

CHAPTER FIVE

Phase 2 (CP) – Control of Paces

La Maîtrise des Allures

THE CONTROL OF PACES is traditionally the second phase of an event and at a two-day competition would normally start off the second day. It is also the phase that appears to be comparatively simple, and is the one that is most often overlooked by many competitors in their preparation for an event. In terms of achievement this is a disastrous thing to do, for careful attention to this phase can give you an opportunity to put one over on your fellow competitors in terms of earning points.

The Control of Paces is conducted in two separate parts – the canter and then the walk, with a maximum of 30 points being awarding for each part of the test.

The objective is first to canter down a normally straight corridor up to 150 metres long. The corridor may not be up to maximum length at some competitions if they have insufficient room, and it may not necessarily be straight. On the majority of occasions, the corridor is about 2 m wide, and is indicated by marking two parallel lines on an area of grassland. Once the canter test is complete, you will be expected to repeat the process in reverse along the same corridor or a very similar one, only this time in walk. The intention is to canter slowly, and walk quickly with your times compared with the scoring table (Appendix 2). The time achieved determines your score, so it is completely objective. However, in either the canter or the walk, failure to stay in the required pace or failure to stay inside the corridor loses you all the marks that you would have achieved in that part of the test.

Preparation and training for this phase has already been covered briefly, but there is still more that you can do when you get to an event.

Make sure that you leave time to walk the CP corridor, so that you can get a feel for the terrain. What initially appears flat may not be so when you walk it. Also, try to imagine how the terrain might have changed by the time it is your turn; not much if you are third to go, but what if there are seventy-three riders ahead of you?

When you walk it for the first time, try to view it through the eyes of your horse. You are the best one to judge if your particular animal is likely to be bothered by anything,

CP – A corridor with extras!

generally off to one side of the track. Many organisers deliberately put something part way down the track and off to one side to test the horses' true level of obedience and training. Even if you think that you have got everything covered, try to take the time to watch other competitors doing their Control of Paces. It can give you a great insight into where the potential pitfalls are, and reveal how something that you had considered perfectly innocuous is the one thing that nearly every horse has decided that it needs to shy at.

Your immediate warming-up routine prior to doing the CP will depend entirely on what works best for you and your horse, but do try and make sure that you do not end up being rushed. Have an established routine to use every time, and aim to make the CP just that – routine. Try not to get tense because this phase is perhaps the 'least' fun, as any tension is likely to be your undoing. One important point to remember: however tempting, this is not the moment to school your horse.

When given the go-ahead to start, don't be rushed into starting prematurely. Make sure that you are relaxed, and your horse is going forward in a calm and balanced manner. The best way to achieve this is on a large circle, slightly away from the start gates, so that when you are happy you can come off the circle smoothly and have sufficient space to approach the start gate in a straight line. The official might begin to get a bit agitated if you take a very long time about this, so aim to be sufficiently organised to achieve this in a relaxed yet efficient manner.

One final word on the approach. Providing you have not crossed the start line between the flags, you have not started the test. So, if something happens to upset you or your horse, such as another competitor crossing in front of you as you make your approach, turn away and begin your approach again.

Once you have started there is no going back, so have a clear picture in your mind about how you are going to ride the track. This may mean riding through the start gate, where there is someone standing with a stopwatch, rather more strongly than you would wish and then allowing the horse to settle into its ideal rhythm. You may have to repeat this process as you approach the finish gate. It is particularly important to keep alert and ride through the finish. So often, judges see a competitor completely relax a few strides before they have crossed through the finish. The horse senses this, and produces a downwards transition, wiping out all the points earned in an instant.

Perhaps it is worth emphasising that a time of 33.8 seconds or above earns you maximum points. With schooling, achieving this time should be perfectly possible for most partnerships without making the test look forced or tense. Some competitors seem to take this test to extremes, putting in times in excess of 40 seconds for the 150 m but producing a test that looks distinctly uncomfortable for both horse and rider. While it makes no difference to the score, try to aim to achieve just enough in a relaxed and harmonious way working with your horse. Often, to strive too hard produces tension, and this is when things can go wrong very quickly.

Once you have ridden through the finish gate in canter, stay on a straight line (if possible), bringing your horse back to walk in a smooth downwards transition. You will need to settle your horse into a relaxed walk rapidly as the judge will expect you to start the walk element of this phase as quickly as possible. Equally, the same advice about preparation holds true for the walk as for the canter. Get your horse settled into a relaxed rhythmical walk before you approach the start gates. Follow the routine etablished in your training at home as you ride through this test, keeping both of you as relaxed as possible. Again, any tension is likely to cause the horse to jog or to slow down by taking short stunted steps, instead of striding out confidently. Keep this relaxed, confident walk going right through the finish gate before rewarding your horse.

Your have now completed Phase 2, and hopefully added another 45+ points to your POR score.

CHAPTER SIX

Phase 3 (PTV) – Obstacles

Parcours en Terrain Varié

IN THE MAJORITY OF COMPETITIONS, you will go straight to the start of the PTV after completing your Control of Paces. The start times given to you for the event will give you a clear indication of how long you have to get to the start of the PTV from the Control of Paces, and normally you should not have to rush to get yourself to the start gate. More often than not, you will have to wait at this point, as it is not unusual for the Control of Paces to overtake the times for the PTV, so an important thing at this point may be for you to concentrate on keeping your horse relaxed, yet alert and warm. If you think that you are going to be held up at this point, and it is a cold or wet day, have an assistant ready with a rug to help prevent your horse getting cold and switching off.

You will have walked the PTV course in advance, so will be familiar with the route, and what you are going to encounter as you go around. Make sure that you can recall the route and the sequence of obstacles easily in your mind. If you can't, or if the PTV course is complicated, you can make a list of simple instructions to serve as an *aide memoire* and tape them to your arm. Sometimes, just a simple note of what direction you should ride away from an obstacle, can stop you taking an uncorrected error of course and losing all your marks for this phase of the competition.

Do remember that while you will know what is coming, your horse will not. It is important to ride every metre positively, transmitting relaxed confidence with every aid to your horse. One of the best ways of doing this is to enjoy the whole PTV course, because your horse will sense your enjoyment of the event, and feed off that.

One of the most important things to do in your preparation during your course walk is to plan the approach to each obstacle carefully. As with nearly all equestrian tests, if you get the approach right, the performance at the obstacle goes well. In the vast majority of instances, things done at the last second upset the horse and produce faults.

You will know the time limit that you have to get around the course. The time limit is set by the official Technical Delegate, once the course has been measured. It is calculated at approximately 12 km/h, but the level of competition, type of terrain, and weather conditions are all taken into account. The length of the course also has a significant influence on the time limit. Basically, doing sixteen obstacles on a long course takes the same amount of time as dealing with sixteen obstacles on a short course, but there is less opportunity to make up the time between the obstacles on a short course. This means that the time set has to be more generous on a short course.

The way the time limit works is that there are no penalties for coming in under the time. Five penalties are awarded for any part of the first minute over the time limit, 15 penalties for any part of the second minute, and 30 penalties for any part of the third minute taken over the time limit. Once a competitor has taken over 3 minutes and earned a total of 30 penalties, no further penalties are awarded.

The time limit set should encourage you to get around the course at a comfortable pace, without having to push on very quickly. A relaxed, forward going canter between the obstacles should bring you in well under the time, providing you have been able to deal with each obstacle in an efficient manner. As soon as you begin to have a problem at an obstacle you will find your leeway in respect of the time limit vanishing rapidly. If you know that there is an obstacle that is likely to cause you a problem, you may need to balance the likely number of points you might earn at that obstacle if things don't go well, against any time penalties you might pick up at the end. Make one quick attempt, and if things don't work, move on around the course (making a mental note that there is some extra work to do at home before the next event).

Again, as with the Control of Paces, make sure that you are sufficiently prepared before setting off. You will know best the degree of warming-up that your horse requires, remembering that in all probability you will only have finished the Control of Paces a short while ago. Find something to jump if you feel it is really necessary, but again remember that you are not about to set off around a cross-country course. There are only likely to be three or four jumps on the course, and you don't want to focus too much attention on them, if jumping your horse in the warm-up area is likely to make it more difficult to do many of the other obstacles that require the horse to be calm and relaxed.

When planning your round, think about relating one obstacle on the course to the next in some detail. How the pattern of obstacles fits together into a whole picture will have a great influence on the outcome of your round. Look at which obstacles follow a jumping obstacle, and at what distance. Will the fact that your horse has just jumped a hedge influence his or her performance in the immobility? Many PTV course designers are fond of putting something like the S-bend at the end of a long section where competitors can be tempted into having a good gallop. It comes as no great surprise that many horses then completely trash the S-bend.

The official rulebook covers twenty-seven obstacles, and at a Championships the sixteen obstacles on the PTV course must be selected from this list. Any of them can be chosen in any order. However, at other competitions don't be surprised if you come across obstacles that have been invented or created for the one event. This is perfectly acceptable within the rules, providing the obstacle tests you in a skill that it is reasonable to expect you to need during a trail ride, and that it is made clear to you how the obstacle is to be judged.

The judging for the PTV is perhaps a little complicated, as it mixes the objective with the subjective. Putting it as simply as possible, up to ten points are awarded at each obstacle, so the maximum score for a PTV round with no time penalties is 160 points. The ten points on each obstacle are generally divided into two separate marks. The first mark is for effectiveness up to a maximum of seven points. You could view this as the mark awarded to the horse. If everything goes smoothly you get seven for effectiveness; if you have one fault or refusal you get four points; and if you have two faults or refusals you get one point. A third problem would give you a zero score for effectiveness, and an overall zero score for that obstacle unless the judge considered that you had ridden dangerously or in a brutal manner. In this case you would be awarded penalties that could give you a minus score for the obstacle.

If you were to have three faults or refusals, earning a zero score, this does not prevent you from continuing on the course. Indeed, if there are any obstacles that you did not want even to attempt, you can opt not to by riding up to the judge and stopping to inform him or her that you will not be attempting the particular obstacle. All this means is that you do not score any points for the obstacle.

The effectiveness score can be topped up to ten with a mark for style.

You could consider this as the mark awarded to you, the rider. Normally, the style mark ranges from plus three to minus two, so you might have jumped the fallen tree effectively (seven points), but your position was only considered 'quite good' by the judge who awarded you one additional point for style, giving you an overall score for that obstacle of eight. A good score, incidentally.

In some of the PTV obstacles, the style mark is determined only by the pace in which you tackled the obstacle. Walking through the obstacle makes it easy, so the style mark would be minus two; trotting through is more challenging earning zero for style; while cantering through requires a considerable degree of skill, earning plus three for style.

At one obstacle (the immobility), the scoring is purely empirical and determined by the stopwatch, as we shall see when looking at that individual obstacle.

A fall on the PTV course as a result of negotiating an obstacle produces a zero score for that obstacle. A second fall on the PTV will produce a zero score for the whole PTV, and you are required to withdraw from the course at that point.

Because there is a degree of subjectivity in most of the judging, you should not be surprised to find that whereas a judge at one event might give you ten points for an obstacle, another judge at a different one might only have given you eight for what you consider has been an indentical performance. Judges will naturally differ in their opinions as to how good something is but, as long as they are consistent in their approach to every rider, this should not change the overall outcome of a particular event.

You will also find that judges do have greater expectations of the rider across the levels, so a performance that would have earned a ten at Level 1, will only get perhaps a seven at Level 4.

Looking at the obstacles listed in the rulebook, they are divided into five basic categories. They are:

(a) **Obstacles where a change of pace is not penalised (chiefly these are jumping obstacles).**
Obstacles falling into this category are:
(1) Ditch (ridden)
(2) Tree trunk
(3) Hedge
(4) Step up (ridden)
(5) Step down (ridden)
(6) Gate

(b) **Obstacles where the pace is 'freestyle' – the mark is not altered whatever pace the riders choose providing that they do not change pace during the obstacle.**

Obstacles falling into this category are:

(7) Riding up an incline

(8) Riding down an incline

(9) Bank

(10) Staircase up (ridden)

(11) Staircase down (ridden)

(12) Reining back

(c) **Obstacles where the pace is set – normally compulsory walk.**

Obstacles falling into this category are:

(13) S-bend test

(14) Footbridge crossing (ridden)

(15) Water crossing

NB: There can be sections of the course where a compulsory pace is stipulated (usually walk) between sets of flags. This is normally done to deal with a particular safety issue.

(d) **Obstacles where the choice of pace (walk, trot or canter) determines the mark – must be canter to earn maximum marks.**

Obstacles falling into this category are:

(16) Bending

(17) Corridor

(18) Low branches

(e) **Led obstacles – dismounted.**

Obstacles falling into this category are:

(19) Leading up an incline

(20) Leading down an incline

(21) Leading up a step

(22) Leading down a step

(23) Ditch (led)

(24) Horse trailer

(25) Footbridge crossing (led)

(26) Immobility

(27) Mounting

Examining these obstacles by category, we begin with those that allow changes in pace.

CATEGORY (a)

All but one involves jumping, or at least may involve jumping. The complete outsider in this list is the gate. The pace you approach or leave the obstacle does not directly affect your score, so to approach in walk and trot away from the obstacle is not considered a change in pace.

The objective in negotiating this obstacle is to retain control of the gate at all times, so that it does not swing open, shut or indeed into the horse on its own. This means that you are required to have hold of the gate at all times from the moment that you grasp hold of the gate to the moment that you refasten it. How a gate fastens will differ from event to event, so it is important to check this when you walk the course. Test it to see if it is easy to unfasten and refasten, to see that it swings both ways or is stiffer when swinging in one direction. Look to see whether you have more room opening the gate one way, or from one direction and check the ground to see if there is anything there that might affect your horse.

PTV – A rider in Western tack starts the gate at a championship event.

Consider your approach carefully, and when you ride the course make sure you approach the gate from the direction that you had intended. It never fails to astound judges at the gate how many riders arrive appearing to have given absolutely no thought as to how they are going to tackle this obstacle. They approach from the shortest direction, and then position themselves initially in such a way as to guarantee that they will have a problem.

Once you have your plan clear in your mind, approach the gate and, having released the latch, try to keep the horse's leading shoulder close to the opening end of the gate. I define the 'leading shoulder' as the one that is near the gate at the end that it opens, as you start the obstacle. Your horse will need to respond to gentle leg aids as you manoeuvre it

through the gate, and put yourself in a position to swing the gate shut (without letting go) and fasten it, with your horse's leading shoulder following the moving end of the gate right the way through the test. If your horse overreacts to your aids, you may well find that you move too far away from the gate and are unable to maintain contact.

One extra word of explanation. It is not a fault, if you are certain that you cannot maintain your grip with one hand, to drop the reins and grasp the gate with that hand before you have to let go with the other. You may lose a point or two for style but not the full three points for a fault in effectiveness.

PTV – A natural hedge grown in an arena, and tackled confidently.

The other obstacles in this category are the jumping ones, and allow for a change of pace. This means you can trot to the obstacle, for example, pop over it and canter away. It is not considered a fault to stop and jump from a standstill providing the horse did not take a step backwards.

The one very slight exception to this is the ridden ditch. Providing the ditch is of a suitable type, and it is safe to do so, there is no requirement

PTV – A ditch taken with confidence: 7 for effectiveness, but a point or two off for style – the rider could have had a better rein contact and 'allowed' more with his hands.

PTV – A versatile and well-built obstacle used as a step down on this occasion.

to jump this obstacle. It is quite OK to walk up to the ditch, scramble down into it and up out the other side and walk away. You have negotiated the obstacle in a safe and effective way, and your score would be calculated in exactly the same way as if you had jumped it.

All the obstacles that involve jumping require single jumping efforts and they are not big. But do remember that they are meant to simulate a problem that you might encounter on a trail ride, so that as long as the take off and landing is safe they may not be sited in as perfect a position as you may naturally wish.

Looking at the judging criteria for the obstacles in this category that involve jumping in slightly more detail, the effectiveness score is largely down to whether you have a refusal, run out or a fall. A fall would give you a zero score for the obstacle, unless there was any question of dangerous riding or brutality involved. These two terms always sound so extreme, but they can cover a multitude of minor misdemeanours.

It is worth pointing out that judges generally use these marks in a way that is meant to be helpful, and as a means of pointing out to a rider areas in which they could improve their performance significantly in the judges' opinion, by adopting a slightly different approach to their riding.

Refusals at a jump will change the effectiveness score in the following way: no refusals = seven points; one refusal = four points; two refusals = one point; and three refusals would give you a zero score for effectiveness and an automatic zero score for the obstacle unless the judge imposed additional penalties for brutality or dangerous riding.

CATEGORY (b)

The next category covers freestyle obstacles. These are obstacles in which you can choose any pace but, having started the obstacle in a particular pace, any change from that would be considered an effectiveness fault. This means a change in the obstacle from canter to trot would drop the effectiveness score from seven to four.

All these obstacles are linear, so you might expect them to be 6–8 m long, if not longer. Clearly, there is an opportunity to change pace in an obstacle that has this degree of depth to it. However, it makes no difference to the number of potential points that you might be awarded whether you tackle the obstacle in walk, trot or canter.

Looking at the obstacles separately, the riding up an incline, and the down, are essentially identical in how they are judged. You should choose your pace clearly in your mind during your course walk and then ride both positively.

Generally, the more impulsion that you have for the ride up, the easier it is to complete this obstacle successfully, so many riders will attack this obstacle in canter providing it is safe to do so. Remember to ride through the finish flags, which can often be sited on the crest of a hill. There is a psychological tendency to pause as horse and rider get to the crest of a hill, so make sure that you don't get fooled into changing pace by this simple trap and ride through the flags.

Most riders prefer to keep firm control on the ride down and stick to walk. This needs regular practice as many horses seem prone to jog, and again the problem can often come at the bottom: horse and rider relax just before crossing through the flags, and jog before the end of the obstacle.

Apart from the change in pace, the other effectiveness fault the judge is looking for is that the horse does not remain in a straight line with the axis of the slope. This will

PTV – The ride down. Stay straight and maintain control, however steep it is. Try not to let the leg slip forward.

PTV – The staircase, essentially the same as the ride up.

require you to keep your horse firmly and evenly between your legs to stop the quarters swinging out of line with the axis of the slope.

The style mark is determined by the balance of the horse and by the position of the rider. Riding firmly and positively, with an effective leg should enable you to maintain good balance and employ your aids effectively to prevent the faults described above.

The bank is a very similar obstacle, but you will need to maintain your chosen pace up the slope, over the crest and down the other side. You will need to be very clear in your mind when you walk the course in which pace it is likely to be possible, and the most effective for you and your horse to complete this entire obstacle.

The staircase, whether up or down, is judged in exactly the same way as the inclines. You will see from the photo above that the design of this obstacle is not to be confused with the type of cross-country jump often referred to as a 'staircase'. This obstacle is literally a flight of stairs and, while it is theoretically possible for you to choose your pace, it is highly likely that everyone is going to opt for the walk. While it is very clearly a fault within the rules to jump up the steps, stepping up more than one at a time is allowed. It is also much easier for you and the judge to know if you have not stayed in line with the axis of the slope, as failure to do so will mean that you will have stepped off the staircase.

The last obstacle in this category allows you to choose any pace in theory but, again in practical terms, you must walk.

The rein back is conducted between two poles placed on the ground and you must rein back between the poles without touching them for a distance of 4 m (maximum). One important point to remember is that while you must enter and exit between the flags, you are only being judged during the rein back itself. This means that you could touch a pole on the way in and trot out once the rein back is completed without incurring a penalty.

The distance for the rein back is quite considerable, being 4 m, but the test is designed to see that you could reverse out of trouble if you had to. The judge, in addition to making sure that you don't touch the edges of the corridor while reining back, will also be looking to see that your horse maintains its progress (part of the effectiveness mark), and that the process is conducted in a relaxed and harmonious fashion (the style mark).

CATEGORY (c)

The third category includes the obstacles where the pace is dictated by the rules.

There are only three ridden obstacles in this category, and the dictated pace is walk. With the first, the S-bend, there is a difference between the *BHS TREC Rulebook* and the international rulebook. The international rulebook does not impose any particular pace but it would be very difficult for anyone to accomplish the S-bend successfully in anything other than walk.

The S-bend is judged on whether the horse touches the sides of the S-

PTV – The S-bend is often dressed as roadworks.

bend, whether it shows any resistance through the changes in direction within the S-bend, and if there is any change in the imposed pace of walk within the obstacle. Possibly the two secrets to getting this obstacle right in a competition is to be very precise about the approach, positioning yourself in the centre of the first lane, and preparing for your first turn early enough. The other important technique is to ride through both turns. Don't try to stop and then try to turn on the forehand, or shift the hindquarters over. This usually leads to a horse knocking a pole in front or behind.

Keeping your horse moving through the turn with impulsion may initially give you the feeling that you are going too fast, but it actually gives you a greater degree of control and allows your horse to maintain its balance.

With the other two obstacles, the footbridge and the water crossing, the pace is imposed chiefly for safety reasons, as

Above:
PTV – The water, negotiated calmly at walk.

Right:
PTV – The bridge, tackled in a confident and relaxed manner.

outside a competition a rider would never come to a strange ford or bridge and canter across without a second thought. The partnership must walk carefully through both these obstacles. A change of pace is an effectiveness fault, although the judge can award no points if she or he considers that the majority of either obstacle was done in a pace other than walk.

Both these obstacles require considerable practice at home. Take advantage of every opportunity to encourage your horse into water when out hacking, so that stepping into water becomes second nature. For the bridge, a bit of board lying on the ground in the stable yard, which can be moved into different positions and has to be walked over every time your horse comes in, will soon get your horse accustomed to stepping onto 'artificial' surfaces.

In competition, it is vital that you give your horse confidence through both these obstacles by maintaining an effective leg contact, and be particularly wary of your horse rushing out of the water or jumping off the bridge at the end.

CATEGORY (d)

The next category is similar to the freestyle category previously discussed but with these obstacles the pace that you choose does affect your score. The other judging criteria for the freestyle obstacles apply equally here, but the style mark is determined only by what pace the obstacle is tackled in, cantering posing a greater challenge and thus earning more points than walk or trot. The style mark for these obstacles can only be minus two for walk, zero for trot or plus three for canter, but the basic concept that a change in pace within the obstacle is an effectiveness fault still applies. So, a change from canter to trot in the obstacle would drop the effectiveness score from seven to four, and the style mark would be determined by the lowest pace, i.e. trot.

The bending, the corridor, and the low branches are the three obstacles covered in this category, and all present a greater challenge when tackled in canter rather than walk or trot. At least, that is the theory, but in actual fact a properly trained horse will perform the corridor and the low branches better in canter than the other paces. Neither the low branches nor the corridor poses a great problem to a horse that is straight, obedient and relaxed.

For the corridor, straightness is everything, as you are expected to pass between two poles or rails on the ground with only a narrow space

PTV – The low branches, taken in canter. Note that the number bib is sticking up above the rider.

between them. Once your horse is suitably trained and has been introduced to this test at home, the two vital things in a competition are to make your approach straight from as far away as possible (up to about 20 m), and to keep your leg firmly and evenly supporting your horse to help keep it straight through the obstacle itself.

One very simple fact to remember is that your horse will probably take more steps in walk or trot to pass down the corridor, than the number of steps taken in canter so by the law of averages you are reducing the risk of hitting the rails by cantering!

For the low branches, cantering again is the best option to take with the trained horse. Walking the horse in hand under the low branches, and then riding under them in walk is fine when introducing a horse to this obstacle. Trotting is rarely a sensible option, except in training under branches set with extra room, as the horse's natural movement is more up and down in trot. Cantering at some speed, once confidence and control are developed, is the best option. The obstacle is over quickly, and a horse allowed to canter develops a longer, lower profile giving you more room to get under the branches.

You need to practise this obstacle with particular regard to your own body position, as in nearly all instances it is the rider who knocks the branches, not the horse. The key to success or failure is going to be your own position. Firstly, your horse must become accustomed to you changing your body position quite dramatically, as you will have to duck forward to avoid hitting the low branches. One of the initial problems you will need to overcome is your movement upsetting the horse's balance, causing him to break pace. This problem is compounded by the likelihood that your lower leg will become insecure and you will not be encouraging your horse forward. The change in your position and the lightening of your leg aid is likely to cause your horse to break pace.

The other problems are more prosaic. Keeping their bottom down can pose a problem for many people. As when jumping, keeping the back flat will help achieve the necessary profile. The other simply rectified problem that often lets people down is loose clothing and/or a number that sticks up. Make sure that you are wearing tight clothing which is not bulky, and that any number bib doesn't stick up above the shoulders or over the back when you crouch forward.

The final obstacle in this section is quite definitely more difficult in canter than in any other pace. The bending poles

PTV — Bending poles. Conducted at trot, this should be a certain 7 points for any rider.

are a series (normally five in a row) of vertical posts placed in a straight line on reasonably level ground, with 5 m between each pole. A corridor marked on the ground indicates the edge of the penalty zone, which runs in a straight line 2 m either side of the line of the poles.

The object is to ride down the line of poles in a serpentine, passing each pole on alternate sides. It does not matter on which side you pass the first pole. You must stay in the same pace from one end to the other. You must not touch any of the poles, and you must not step outside the corridor down which the line of poles runs. If you break pace, touch a pole or step outside the corridor, this is judged as an effectiveness fault and marked accordingly. The style mark is determined by the pace, as previously described in this section.

Very rarely are the bending poles walked, as this is a simple exercise. Equally, not many competitors are able to tackle this successfully in canter, as it does require a well-schooled horse with a very balanced canter to cope with this. The vast majority of competitors play safe and go for the comparatively easy seven points for trotting through this obstacle.

CATEGORY (e)

The final category in this simple breakdown covers the led obstacles. All these are designed to show that the horse is safe to work and lead from the ground, and is just as responsive and obedient as when ridden. Some of the obstacles are intended to test you with a very specific problem (such as the immobility), and some are more general in their purpose, checking to see that you are safe in the method that you use, and that the horse responds sensibly (such as leading through a trailer).

Two general points are worth remembering. If you ride with a running martingale, which is allowed by the rules, you must not lead from the reins. You should have a headcollar and lead rope to enable you to lead safely. The other point to remember is that for all the dismounted exercises, you should have stirrups run up or crossed over to avoid them swinging about. Failure to do this will earn you a penalty point, even if you cross them over and they fall loose during the test.

The first two obstacles, which can be looked at together, are the lead up and lead down. They are judged in an identical way and, with regard to the style mark, quite differently from any of the other led obstacles. The judge will look at the general conduct of the whole test when assessing style, but will also be looking very carefully at the position of the rider while leading the horse.

The object of this test is to see whether the combination could negotiate a narrow path or track when for some reason it is not possible for the horse to be ridden. This means that the horse must be led safely and willingly from in front. So, the basis for the style mark is determined by from where the horse is led. If the dismounted rider is in front of the horse, the maximum style mark could be three points; level with the head two points; level with the shoulder one point; level with the girth zero points; level with the hindquarters minus one; and behind the horse minus two points.

If the whole test is performed without tension, and the rider does not have to drag the horse up or down the slope, this will also be reflected in the style mark.

The effectiveness mark covers the following faults:

- the horse not staying in line with the axis of the slope;

- the horse bumping into the rider;

- the rider allowing the reins or lead rope to touch the ground;

- the horse refusing to follow the rider or getting loose;

- stepping out of the marked corridor (if there is one).

It is worth stressing that if you are not entirely sure about leading your horse from in front, it is best to accept that you will lose one or two style marks and lead from beside the head or shoulder, than risk having an accident.

The next group of leading obstacles, which can be grouped together, are the leading up a step, leading down a step, ditch, horse trailer and the

footbridge crossing. Essentially, all of these test the basic attributes of the horse while it is being led and in particular that it behaves sensibly, safely and follows the instructions of the dismounted rider. The rider is expected to carry out the required test safely.

PTV – The led ditch. This pair look relaxed. The shoulders of both horse and rider are facing forward and they are moving positively through the obstacle.

When negotiating the steps and the ditch, it is quite acceptable to use a long lead rein, and get up or down the step, or across the ditch while your horse waits for you, before following on your instruction. However, if you have to return to your horse in order to motivate it to follow you, this would be deemed a fault and the effectiveness score would drop from seven to four. Equally, if your horse takes a step backwards, this is also viewed as a disobedience and your effectiveness score would be altered accordingly.

It is important to be careful to make sure that you do not put yourself into a position where your horse might jump into you, and the best way to avoid this happening is to train at home, so you are entirely familiar with how your horse might react in most situations.

The horse trailer should be a front unload, with no partition and the simple requirement is to lead your horse up into the trailer and straight out of the front. There is no requirement to stop inside the trailer, and the judge will be looking to see that the whole process is conducted smoothly and safely, without anyone knocking into the trailer and without your horse rushing through. Once out of the trailer, unless you are to continue dismounted onto another obstacle, there is usually nothing to prevent you from using the ramp to remount.

The footbridge is pretty much as the above, although you must be careful to walk across the footbridge. You should also be careful that neither you nor your horse steps off the bridge.

The final two obstacles covered in this book are in many ways the most unusual, and one of them seems to cause riders more trouble than any other.

The first of these oddballs is the immobility. This is designed to test that your horse will stand without being held or tied up, to allow you to deal with a possible problem such as opening a difficult gate on a trail. Normally, the immobility is conducted within a pen of some description so that the organisers don't end up with loose horses charging around the PTV. The obstacle is made up of two concentric circles marked on the ground, the inner one having a 4 m diameter, and the outer one an 8 m diameter.

The aim is to get your horse to stay within the 4 m circle while you stand just outside the 8 m circle. Manage this for 10 seconds and you will have earned ten points. However, it is not quite so straightforward. Firstly, you only have 10 seconds to position your horse in the inner circle. The timing for this begins when your horse first steps into the inner circle and, unless you are outside the outer circle within 10 seconds, you will not score any points whatsoever regardless of whether your horse stands perfectly within the circle.

While you are positioning your horse, after leaving the inner circle but before stepping outside the outer circle, there are two opportunities to reposition your horse should it attempt to follow you. Remember, you will be burning up your 10 seconds to get out of the outer circle and each intervention counts as an effectiveness fault and reduces the maximum number of points you can score. Ten points is the maximum, seven points if you make one intervention, four for a second intervention and zero points for the obstacle if you make a third intervention. You would almost certainly have used up your 10 seconds anyway, so this is largely academic.

Once you have stepped outside the outer circle, you can do nothing more and your score will be determined by the amount of time that your horse stays inside the inner circle. It may move around and graze but the timing stops the moment it touches the line or steps over it. You may ground tie with split reins or a lead rope. Otherwise, the reins should be left on the neck, and the only aid you can use is your voice.

If your horse stands perfectly still – as many do – you should have no problem leaving the reins on the neck. However, if you think your horse is going to move around and there might be a risk of the reins slipping forward and the horse stepping on them, you should secure them to the saddle.

Finally, we come to the British rider's *bête noir*, the mount. The aim of this test is simply to show that the rider can easily mount the horse from the ground, and from either side. The horse must stand still to allow the rider to mount with full control. The mount must be completed within 15 seconds, with the horse standing perfectly still inside a small (2.5 m diameter) circle marked on the ground. If the horse moves one foot while the rider is mounting, that is deemed to be an effectiveness fault, dropping the score from a potential seven to four. If the horse steps out of the circle before the rider has mounted, that would be a zero score in total.

The timing for this obstacle starts the moment the horse steps into the circle, and finishes when the rider has both feet in the stirrups. Any time taken over the 15 seconds is converted into penalty points and deducted from the score, so a rider undertaking this obstacle perfectly and getting ten points, but taking 25 seconds (10 seconds over the time allowed) would end up on a zero score.

Riders are permitted to use stirrup extensions, providing that they carry them on the entire PTV, and in this case the timing finishes when the stirrup extensions are safely stowed away.

When you walk the PTV course, look carefully at the circle and plan

PTV – The mount. Equally easy, whichever side.

your approach just as meticulously as for any other obstacle. Ask yourself, 'Is the circle on a slight slope that might give me an advantage when mounting; are there any distractions around the circle which might affect my horse?' You have two basic options.

You can ride into the circle, dismount and remount immediately. This is a very straightforward option for you, but the chances are that the mount will come at the end of a number of dismounted obstacles and you will be approaching the mounting circle on foot. Prepare yourself properly before you enter the circle, so that you have little to do other than get on once you have entered the circle and triggered the timing. However, you cannot lower your stirrups prior to entering the circle as this will incur one penalty point.

Once you are in the circle, make sure that your horse is standing squarely and evenly balanced on all four legs before you attempt to mount. If your horse is not standing square, it is highly likely to move a leg as you mount to accommodate your weight. You need to mount as quickly as possible and not waste time having to search to get your 'free' foot into a stirrup. You want to mount as lightly as possible, as this will give you a better style mark.

As with all these obstacles, for the majority of people mounting from the ground from either side becomes easy with practice. If you do not make your horse stand still at home when you mount, it is unreasonable to expect it to stand still when you get on at a competition. Equally, you need to train yourself both physically and mentally to do this. If you need to, create an artificial opportunity to train yourself before you inflict this on your horse.

However, there is no getting away from the fact that if you suffer from any lack of mobility, or you are short and have a very big horse you are always going to struggle with this obstacle. Having accepted that, you will realise that just about every TREC competitor has an obstacle that either they or their horse struggles at, and it may be at something that you find ludicrously easy.

This is one of the great attractions of TREC: it allows for the fact that while we may strive for perfection, perfection is never achievable. By testing horse and rider across a broad range of skills, it acts as a great leveller, so that a very wide range of riders can compete together with an equal chance of success.

ADDITIONAL PTV TRAINING TIPS

Quite a bit about training has already been said in the section on the PTV, but these additional general tips will help you plan and develop your training. Try not to view the advice offered in this book as a conclusion, but use it to stimulate your own thoughts about how to prepare for a competition, and more importantly how to make your horse a better saddle horse.

Generally, with the right mental attitude, you and your horse can learn from every situation that you find yourselves in, so try to look at everything as a positive learning opportunity. Specifically, there are many things you can do to train for the PTV without needing much equipment. A sheet of board lying flat on the ground (and moved into different places) can get your horse perfectly used to walking over a footbridge.

With all the obstacles involving poles or bars on the ground, make the space between the bars greater than the dimensions listed in *The BHS TREC Rulebook*, so that the horse has more room to learn what is expected of it to start with.

For the S-bend, start initially with only three poles on the ground, so that your horse only has to make a single turn to the left or the right, and can clearly see an exit route. Gradually add in the rest of the poles progressively. Make it your objective to ride through the whole obstacle, keeping the forward momentum going throughout, albeit slowly at the corners. Stopping and trying to turn on the forehand or on the haunches is likely to result in your dislodging a pole. Far better to keep moving forward, as then your horse will find it easier to manoeuvre, and even big horses will try to avoid knocking the poles if they possibly can.

For the corridor obstacle, begin with the poles placed on the ground

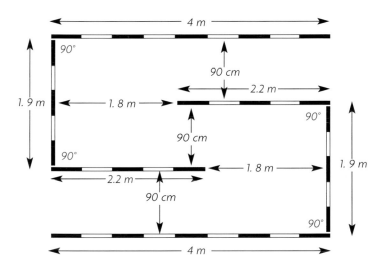

Example S-bend layout.

at least 80 cm apart and as your training progresses make the corridor narrower. Introduce distractions such as plant pots or dustbins off to one side of the corridor. Anything like this should not deflect your horse from the job you are asking him or her to do. That's the theory, at least. The vital thing with this obstacle is to keep your horse straight, as any bend may result in the horse stepping wide with one foot and striking a pole.

The rein back is arguably the most difficult obstacle to perform, but remember its purpose – to enable you to back out of a difficult situation. There are two things to work on here, and don't leave it until a competition to discover if your horse will rein back. Far better to miss this obstacle than get your horse in a muddle and upset its first experience on the PTV course.

The first thing you need to establish is that your horse understands what you are asking. By creating forward impulsion but not allowing your horse to move forward, it can easily become confused. It can be a great help to have an assistant on the ground who encourages the horse to step backwards while you give the aids. Once any initial confusion is cleared up about what your aids mean, you can progress quickly. The other very important element to establish right from the beginning is straightness. In a competition, you will be asked to step backwards for 4 m without pausing between two poles just 80 cm apart lying on the ground without touching them. Your horse is going to have to trust you implicitly, as it cannot see behind itself, and needs to believe that it is OK to step backwards if you say it is.

To train for this, first try to create a situation where your 'rein back corridor' has sides. You may be very fortunate in having some buildings where there is a narrow passageway suitable to use for this purpose. Even a one-sided corridor such as the side of a building, a fence or a hedge can help you get started. You can create your own 'corridor' using show jumps with four jump stands and two poles. Set the poles at about stifle height first, and have the corridor about 1.5 m wide. This will greatly help your horse to understand that it must reverse between two 'walls'. As your training progresses, gradually reduce the width of the corridor and the height of the walls, until the exercise can be performed efficiently with the poles on the ground.

For the jumping obstacles, the best advice is to work with your instructor or coach on basic techniques. Almost certainly in any competition, the jumps are likely to be smaller than you anticipate but are often presented in slightly awkward circumstances. In training, the key areas to work on are to get your horse used to jumping an obstacle from only a short approach, and to focus on jumping straight and accurately, as on occasions the obstacles can be narrow.

Don't spend your time concentrating on getting your horse to jump bigger, but get it used to jumping things other than the traditional looking fence. Rather than raising the height of your jump, put some unusual 'clutter' (providing it does not create a dangerous situation) around your fence or even under the pole that you are jumping. A coat or blanket put over a jump pole can turn a plain fence into something that requires considerably more thought from your horse.

In a competition, your main responsibility will be to get the approach right. If you manage this, almost certainly your horse is more likely to jump well. The straighter you can get the approach and the more time your horse has to see the obstacle, the greater your chance of getting a good score. And in TREC, the jumping obstacles involve single jumping efforts rather than combinations.

For the leading exercises, get your horse used to being worked from the ground. When introducing any new challenge it can be of great benefit to lead your horse through what is required of it before you ride. This serves two purposes. Your horse has the opportunity to take its own time to become familiar with something new, and it gets used to tackling a test without you on its back.

The ideal that you are looking for is that your horse should come to respect your personal space and would never think of bumping into you or stepping on your toes, but is willing to be led through a range of unusual situations by you, the senior partner. Horses that were long reined extensively as part of their training as youngsters seem to take to tackling tests without a rider without any apprehension.

And don't just concentrate on the specific problems listed in the TREC rulebook. Invent different situations for you and your horse to tackle on foot, so that you become more confident that your horse will deal with something strange, and your horse develops more trust in you.

For the mount, which often comes at the end of one or two led obstacles, you must have trained your horse to stand still. Again, this should not be something confined to a competition, but should be at the core of every horse's training as a youngster. A horse that moves as the rider is trying to mount is more than a nuisance. And, this applies equally if you are mounting from the ground or with assistance. Never let your horse move when you are mounting. If it does, start again. If it stays still, make sure that you are generous with your praise so that it clearly understands what you are seeking.

For yourself, make sure that you can deal with the physical effort of mounting from both sides. If you have a problem getting on from the ground anyway, it is likely that this is always going to present you with a bit of a problem, but some physical training can still produce a degree of improvement. Some work on your own mobility and flexibility will benefit both you and your horse while you ride, even if you have no intention of ever attempting this obstacle in an event.

If you can mount comfortably from the ground on the near side, you should be able to do it just as comfortably from the off side. You just need to get your body responding equally, and develop the strength to be 'two-sided'. Generally, this will help with your physical co-ordination, what-ever you are doing, and will benefit your horse when you are riding too.

Providing you can find a suitable gate (preferably not someone else's that you are likely to break), training to improve your ability to mount can be easy and progressive. Using the part of the gate nearest the hanging post, simply practise climbing over the gate, first leading with the right leg then with the left. As you progress, you should notice that it becomes more difficult for you to remember which leg it is easier for you to lead with. You can also use this to help develop your muscles, by starting with a small step up onto the gate with your leading leg. Gradually, make your first step onto the gate higher as your muscles become more used to the effort.

All these tips are simple to follow and should make entry into TREC even easier for you than it already is. They should also help sow the seeds in your mind that will develop your own ideas for training.

Conclusion

TREC IS PERHAPS UNIQUE amongst equestrian disciplines, as its ultimate goal is not a specific sporting outcome. For most sports, the result supersedes the performance in terms of importance, and places the greatest emphasis on 'defeating' the opposition. The vast majority of riders across all the disciplines do put their relationship with their horse at the pinnacle of their sport, but results still count for a great deal. While all TREC riders enjoy the sensation of success, most get far more out of the sport because of the places it takes them to, and because of the opportunity it gives them to spend extended periods of time working with their horse. Through this, they have the opportunity to develop a very special relationship with their horse, something often denied the average recreational rider.

Talking to people who have made extended journeys on horseback, most suggest that only after a number of days spent in the saddle do horse and rider begin to truly gel together. TREC begins to assist riders in developing this sense of partnership based, not on formal instruction and the conscious use of the aids, but on a sub-conscious two-way connection between two living creatures, through what could best be termed as subtle non-verbal communication.

It is often remarked that great jockeys (in any discipline) are able to communicate with their horses in a way that is undetectable to the watcher, as though the horse is telepathic or has some other mystical way of communicating. The truth is more mundane, but the results can be the same and can be achieved by the vast majority of riders. Horses have survived as prey animals by being able to pick up messages from other creatures. Being able to detect whether the creature heading in your direction is eyeing you up as dinner long before it has reached your side, can be a big plus if you are a horse.

Being in physical contact with a rider, the horse's receptors pick up our messages far earlier than we realise, so it is by no means unusual for a rider simply to think about a change in pace for it to happen. This is not telepathy. The horse has picked up the beginnings of the rider's message through sub-conscious changes in the rider's body as he or she prepares to transmit the message. This is quite enough for the trained horse to respond to, and to the observer it appears that horse and rider move as one. Thus TREC can open the door to true partnership.

Usefully, TREC can be a comfortable adjunct to any other discipline. It develops fitness and stamina in both horse and rider, which can help underpin any other activity. It can form a great basis for the general education and physical development of young horses, giving them an early opportunity to experience an organised sport, before tackling something where the physical and intellectual demands become greater. For the older competition horse, it offers a less demanding outlet for its competitive nature, so retirement does not become a trial of boredom. And for all horses, it helps develop the skills and attitudes which the vast majority of riders need from their horses most of the time. It is a sport where the benefit really does lie in taking part, not in the winning, and as such the best thing about TREC is getting out there and doing it!

APPENDIX I

LEVELS OF COMPETITION

(Extracted from the official BHS rulebook, third edition)

Level	POR length	CP	PTV heights*	Championships
One	Up to 12kms	Up to 150m	Approx. 60cm	Up to 10% more (POR)
Two	Up to 20kms	Ditto	Approx. 70cm	
Three	Up to 32kms	Ditto	Approx. 80cm	Up to 10cm higher (PTV)
Four	Up to 40kms	Ditto	Approx. 90cm	

*Heights of any jumping obstacles on the PTV.

At any level it is possible to divide classes into Series A and B. Series A would denote a more technically demanding POR phase than Series B, but the other phases could be run over the same course.

Only at LEVEL THREE or upwards, and with prior warning, might the POR phase include a night-time section.

At level THREE and above competitors should be prepared to use grid references (eight figure) and/or bearings only for the purposes of navigation.

Appendix 2

Control of paces markings

(Extracted from the official BHS rulebook, third edition)

MARK	WALK	CANTER
	time in seconds	*time in seconds and tenths of a second*
30	67 and less	33.8 or more
29	68	33.6
28	69	33.5
27	70	33.3
26	71	33.2
25	72	33
24	73	32.9
23	74	32.7
22	75	32.6
21	76	32.4
20	77	32.3
19	78	32.1
18	79	32
17	80	31.8
16	81	31.7
15	82	31.5
14	83	31.4
13	84	31.2
12	85	31.1
11	86	30.9
10	87	30.8
9	88	30.6
8	89	30.5
7	90	30.3
6	91	30.2
5	92	30
4	93	29.3
3	94	28.5
2	95	27.8
1	96	27
0	97	26.3

Appendix 3

Equipment list for BHS TREC competitions

(Extracted from the official BHS rulebook, third edition)

The following is required for all levels of competition. Additional items may be included for your own comfort.

Competition Compulsory Equipment (for all riders in all phases)
- a hard hat complying with current standards (BSEN 1384, PAS 015 or ASTM F1163) and bearing the kite mark or SEI (correct at time of printing)
- safe and appropriate clothing and footwear * (see note)

POR Compulsory Equipment (for all riders)
(Penalties will be incurred for missing items)
- Compass
- Pens (for map marking – ideally two colours, permanent ink with thin nibs, red and fluorescent orange are popular and black or blue for notes)
- Torch (lightweight – sufficient to read map – a head torch is ideal)
- First aid equipment both equine and human – e.g. bandage, saline solution, sterile dressing, wound powder
- Waterproofs (jacket)
- Whistle (for use in emergencies)
- Headcollar and leadrope or combination bridle
- Emergency farriers tools (suitable for the removal of a shoe and nails) and equi-boot or similar (only compulsory at Level 3 & above)
- Personal ID – minimum requirement, rider name, rider number and emergency telephone number.
- ID on Horse – minimum requirement, rider number and emergency telephone number.
- Fluorescent/reflective high-viz clothing. The minimum requirement is clearly visible fluorescent strips (or garment) on the rider's torso. It is strongly recommended that this is also reflective, and is supplemented by a fluorescent/reflective hatband.
- Pairs competitors must have all the compulsory items between them unless advised otherwise. However, they must EACH have hard hat, fluorescent clothing, waterproofs, headcollar/rope and a whistle and are encouraged to carry the full list if possible.

List continues overleaf

Also helpful for the POR phase
– A map case
– Saddle bags (or suitable alternative)
– Coins and/or mobile phone for emergency phone call
– Telephone numbers to call (supplied by organiser)
– Drink and snack for rider
– Digital watch or stopwatch

Note* For this competition experience has shown that footwear with a tread sole and 1/2 chaps are more suitable than the conventional Riding Boot. Bearing in mind that a lot of the time can be spent dismounted leading your horse over rough terrain up and down hill. Footwear without a clear heel, such as, running shoes (similar to those worn by foot orienteers and Endurance riders) may be used during the POR phase but must be used with a suitable stirrup with cage.
It is recommended that a medical armband is worn during every phase.

APPENDIX 4

BRITISH EQUESTRIAN TOURISM QUALIFICATIONS

These qualifications were especially developed for those working in the equestrian tourism industry, particularly those taking out treks/trail rides/hacks to provide industry relevant, recognised standards at three levels – Assistant Ride Leader, Ride Leader and Riding Holiday Centre Manager,

These three levels of qualification are recognised throughout the British Isles, and are jointly awarded by the British Horse Society (BHS), and the Association of Irish Riding Establishments (AIRE), the Trekking and Riding Society of Scotland (TRSS), and the Welsh Trekking and Riding Association (WTRA). The BHS Is the Secretariat for these qualifications and further information about them can be obtained from the Society.

The Ride Leader and Riding Holiday Centre Manager certificates are internationally recognised and accredited by FITE (Fédération Internationale de Tourisme Equestre) and successful candidates also receive a FITE certificate.

The FITE was founded in 1975 to promote and develop equestrian tourism, and encourage international co-operation for the benefit of individuals and member states, and for the benefit of the public in general.

The FITE represents members' interests with national and international authorities on all questions relating, whether directly or indirectly, to equestrian tourism.

The FITE seeks to raise the awareness of equestrian tourism by developing relevant and suitable qualifications for the industry – the BTEC qualifications at Ride Leader and Centre Manager are accredited by the FITE – to promote the industry as safe and well regulated with the public, making equestrian tourism more accessible to an ever-widening group.

Appendix 5

Useful Addresses

BHS TREC
Competitions Office
The British Horse Society
Stoneleigh Deer Park
Kenilworth
Warwicks
CV8 2XZ
tel: 01926 707831 fax: 01926 707796
competitions@bhs.org.uk   www.bhs.org.uk

British Equestrian Federation
National Agricultural Centre
Stoneleigh Park
Kenilworth
Warwicks
CV8 2RH
tel: 0247 669 8871 fax: 0247 669 6484
info@bef.org.uk   www.bef.org.uk

Fédération Internationale de Toursime Equestre
9 Boulevard Macdonald
75019 Paris
France
tel: (0)145 088860   fax: (0)145 229619
c.detavernier@chevalunic.fr   www.fite-net.org